A Sir
Twist of Faith

LEAH SCHIERMEYER

ACKNOWLEDGMENTS

Most importantly, I want to thank the Almighty for His faithfulness and unconditional love. His kindness endures forever.

I also want to thank my husband for his support and guidance in this endeavor.

I wish to express a very special thanks to Rebbetzen Simmy Wagner and Mrs. Felicia Herscovici for encouraging me not to give up and to tell my story.

Also, a special "thank you" to Rebbetzen Lori Palatnik who offered the following advice when I told her I could not write: "just get it down."

Special appreciation goes to Rebbetzen Sarah Shapiro who had enough confidence in me to publish an excerpt of my story in her latest book, "All Our Lives."

In addition, a special note of gratitude to Rabbi Menachem Lehrfield for his professional assistance in typesetting and cover design.

May Hashem reward all those individuals who gave of their time and energy to help with the publishing of this book. You have my boundless appreciation.

PREFACE

When my husband and I first started questioning our lifetime traditional beliefs in Christianity, the response from others was shock, disdain, and overwhelming avoidance. I desperately wanted answers to what I considered very haunting questions. The underlying question of "could Christianity actually be wrong?" became a frightening and all-consuming thought for me. We consulted pastors, lay leaders, family members, and read books dedicated to answering "the hard questions." Yet, ultimately, no one seemed to have the answers we needed. I felt as though my husband and I were the only people on the planet who, as serious and devoted Christians, had ever questioned Christianity. I felt desperate and embarrassed. I searched, in vain, for books about individuals who had perhaps encountered similar experiences. I wanted to read about how someone had experienced the same thoughts and feelings and challenges that I had experienced. I wanted someone to whom I could relate.

Because I have now been privileged to experience the real beauty and truth of Judaism, I would like to share my journey. This book is dedicated to all of those who perhaps have experienced some of the same challenges I encountered, as well as to those friends who would always say, "you really ought to write a book." Well, I did . . . and here's my story.

1

It's been said, "Everyone has a story." If you were to have asked me as a young girl to write a script for my life, it would have read quite differently than my life today. Of course, perhaps everyone says that—I don't know. What I do know is that I have a story to tell in hopes that it may help others along the same path.

You may ask, "How did a country girl like me, a Baptist, and raised in the middle of the Oklahoma Bible Belt, become an observant Jew?" Well, it's a long story, with many twists and turns, but one that many have asked to hear. Here is my story . . .

To begin with, I was raised in a Missionary Baptist church. Missionary Baptists believe in the total inerrancy of the Bible—both "Old" and "New". They believe there is only one way to heaven, which is through faith in Jesus, and only those who have a true faith and manifest it in their lives will be "saved". The Baptist church frowned upon smoking, drinking, dancing, playing cards, or any frivolous revelry. Those engaging in such activities probably were not "saved," according to the church. My great grandfather was a Baptist minister. All of his children and grandchildren, including my father, followed steadfastly in his footsteps. As early as I can remember, my family attended church regularly. The first church I remember attending was a very small country church in Oklahoma, just a mile up the hill west from my house. It had a wooden floor that my mother mopped faithfully every Saturday before Sunday services, two outhouses in the back, two study classrooms, and a small sanctuary. The congregation was small, probably no more than 50 regular members. My Sunday School teacher was Mrs. Williams. She was a kind grandmother who would give me LifeSavers and Dentyne gum for sitting quietly and listening in her class. The pastor was Brother Joseph, a

Jew who had left his faith to embrace Christianity. I remember very little about him other than he was blind and carried a cane. I also remember very little about the actual services other than we attended every week and that "Brother Doyle" would always turn around to smile and wink at me when everyone else's eyes were supposed to be closed for prayer.

When I was six years of age, the small church disbanded and most families moved from the country to surrounding towns and joined other churches. My parents and my older sibling, Norris, joined Broadway Heights Baptist Church in Clinton, Oklahoma, about a 25 mile drive from our house. We continued living in the country, but would make the drive every Sunday morning and Sunday evening, and sometimes Wednesday evening, to attend services. This was no small feat, considering there were cows to milk and farm chores to take care of in the morning and evening before making the drive to church. I remember feeling awkward, at first, because I was shy and knew none of the other kids my age. One Sunday morning, though, as the envelope was being passed around the Sunday School class for kids to drop in their "giving" (or tzedekah in Jewish terms), I was ignored, as usual, and the envelope continued to be passed around me. One girl, named Leslie, called out, "Well, don't just pass it around her! Let her have it, too!" I adored her-- such a small gesture on her part, but such a huge impact on me. She made sure that I was included and that I had someone to sit with in church. She invited me and my family to her house for Sunday lunch, and sometimes, dessert on Sunday evenings. She invited me to play at her house, which appeared, to me, to be a mansion. She was the nicest girl I had ever met. When she smiled, her face lit up highlighting her short, sandy blonde hair and cute freckles. She was definitely the most popular girl at church and at school. And best of all, she was my friend. I began to look forward to attending church every week. The teachings of Broadway Heights Baptist Church made an indelible impression upon my heart and soul.

I remember one particular Sunday, when as a child, I was sitting in class and a dark-haired, dark-eyed boy raised his hand to ask a question as Sunday School class began. The teacher, Mr. Williams, called on him. "Mr. Williams, if people have to believe in Jesus to be saved, what did people do in the Old Testament before he was born?"

"Well, that's a good question. Back then, the people didn't have Jesus yet, so they just believed that he was going to be born, and looked forward to it, and that's how they were saved."

That question remained with me for many, many years. So, even though the "Old Testament" people didn't know about Jesus yet, all they had to do was believe he was going to be born and that's how they were "saved"? They didn't pray any special prayers. They didn't have any specific scriptures saying

"I will send my son to die on a cross for you for your sins", yet they were supposed to still believe in Jesus, look forward to his birth, and by that belief, have a part in the World to Come. That did not make sense to me.

However, I liked the people and respected the pastor and the teachings of the church immensely. My father and mother were both Sunday School teachers. My father also was a church soloist and often led the congregation in church worship. My brother served as piano accompanist for the youth group and I enjoyed active participation in the church.

I was "saved" at the early age of nine. The pastor always preached the importance of being saved. It was taught that if anyone—including myself—were to die without believing in Jesus, they would die and burn in hell forever and forever. It was an incredibly scary, haunting thought indeed. Oftentimes, the pastor would speak of the horrible eternal details of hell: the fiery furnace, the insatiable thirst, the incredible loneliness, and the overwhelming sorrow one would feel for not believing in God's son, Jesus. And it would be FOREVER. He would also preach of the incredible suffering Jesus endured on the cross and how that anyone who would reject Jesus would also be rejecting God himself. Even though I prayed at age nine for Jesus to come into my heart, I found myself praying the same prayer over and over—just to make sure—that I had done it correctly because if I hadn't done it correctly or had enough faith, the consequences were indeed dire, to say the least.

This was not the only teaching, but it was the foundational teaching upon which everything else was based. I was also taught to live a good, moral, upright life, but that was to be a by-product of my faith in Jesus. One of the tools for measuring whether or not someone was really a Christian was by how he/she lived their life. I wanted to make sure that I lived my life correctly —not just so others would judge me favorably, but because I wanted a part in the world to come, and more importantly, a relationship with God, my creator and ultimate King of the Universe.

I attended church regularly at Broadway Heights until I began college in 1975. I then joined First Baptist Church in Weatherford, Oklahoma, my hometown. It was a much shorter drive and boasted a huge population of college students. The preaching was dynamic and I had an increasing desire to grow spiritually. Besides preaching about the importance of a relationship with Jesus, the pastor taught practical applications for daily living. His sermons proved to be very inspirational, as evidenced by the growing church attendance. I was delighted to be a Christian and a member of such a growing, vibrant church.

The church was a vital part of my life and my family. I attended church every week—religiously. Just as my parents and grandparents were totally committed to a God-centered life, I too, wanted that for myself. My parents taught me that God loved me, mainly by their own example of faith, and that there are strong consequences for the choices we make.

My parents worked extremely hard to make a living and to provide for me and my brother. Money was often scarce for us, but my parents' generosity outweighed materialism. Their principles of honesty, hard work, and a faith in God were evident to all those who knew them. My mother sewed all my clothes, raised an enormous vegetable garden that sustained us throughout the entire year, and helped my father with the farm chores which included tending to the cows, chickens, pigs, and crops of wheat and cotton. The farm life never brought us much wealth, but my parents were always eager to provide free fresh fruits and vegetables, along with fresh dairy products at a minimal price, for every neighbor within a 10 mile radius.

I lived on the farm with my parents for 22 years. After graduating from college with a degree in Office Administration, I finally moved out on my own and began my first job, working as an administrative assistant for the local 3M Company. The job was challenging and rewarding, but dating prospects were extremely limited. My small hometown did not consist of a large population of young, eligible single men. After five years of working with 3M, at age 27, I searched for a job in Oklahoma City, hoping to expand my horizons to include more job opportunities--and more men. I ended up accepting a job as an administrative assistant with Fidelity Bank in downtown Oklahoma City. I also began attending Council Road Baptist Church. It was a huge metro church, boasting more than 1,000 members. The church had a thriving singles group, and as unspiritual as it may sound, was one of the main attractions for me at the time. I dated a few young men at the church, but none of them seemed to be "the one" . . . until one fateful evening.

2

It was early April. I happened to get lost, trying to deliver some home-baked brownies to the apartment of Chuck Gagetta. Chuck was hosting the single men's Bible Study on a Thursday evening and at his request, I offered to bring over some brownies. Chuck's girlfriend, Peggy, happened to be one of my very good friends. Either she gave me wrong directions or I misunderstood them, but I ended up at the wrong apartment. (I guess I should know by now: everything is for the good.) Not knowing what to do next, I walked back to my car, hoping someone I knew would soon show up and I could have them direct me to Chuck's apartment. Within minutes, a svelte young gentleman drove up in his crème-colored Olds 88 and started walking around my car, a Bible in his hand. I didn't know him, but I figured "how many men would be walking around with a Bible in hand unless they're going to the Bible study?"

I quickly jumped out of my car and hollered, "Excuse me, are you going to the men's Bible Study?"

He didn't say too much, just nodded.

"Could you show me where Chuck's apartment is located?"

Again, he didn't say too much, just motioned straight ahead. As we walked, he introduced himself. "Hello, I'm Bob Schiermeyer."

I smiled, "I'm Marcella Payne and I'm supposed to take these brownies to Chuck and somehow I got lost."

Bob soon directed me to Chuck's apartment where I quickly placed the brownies on the kitchen counter and left to meet my friend Peggy for dinner.

At church the next Sunday, Bob approached me and gave me an empty brownie platter. I thought it rather odd that he was concerned with returning the platter to me, rather than Chuck, but then again, it was a nice gesture. Then, on Monday, I received the following phone call:

"Is this the woman who bakes the delicious brownies?"

"I think so," I replied. "Who is this?" I asked.

"Well, this is Bob Schiermeyer." He was actually calling to ask me out for an evening. I was reluctant at first, thinking his youthful appearance made him much younger than me (turns out he is actually three years older), and that I didn't know enough about him. However, I soon learned that he was president of the singles group in his church in Wichita, Kansas, that he was currently a pilot in the Air Force, and that he was now in Oklahoma City, preparing for the MCAT test for medical school. I reasoned anyone who was a Christian, the leader of a singles group, a pilot, and wanted to be a doctor couldn't be all that bad—he actually might be pretty interesting. Therefore, I agreed to an evening out with him. We spent our first evening, eating KFC chicken at the park, and getting to know each other better. Bob, being the methodical person he is, actually had a questionnaire for me to answer, but in some ways, I was flattered that he was so organized for our first date! We spent many hours talking that evening.

Our courtship was a short one—only seven months. We discussed many topics during that time. However, the topic of kosher food almost threatened to end our relationship. Bob drove to Oklahoma City one evening, after his alert duty at McConnell Air Force Base, to eat dinner with me. I had prepared, what I thought was a scrumptious meal, and was anxious to spend more time with him. However, shortly after he arrived at my front door, he commented, "You know, Wayne, my roommate, and I have been doing some studying about the Jewish dietary laws and we don't know the reason for many of them, but we decided it's probably a pretty good idea to try and follow them as much as possible."

I had prepared baked ham for dinner. It was not cheap and I was not impressed that Bob ate the other food, but left the ham untouched. The next morning, he arrived early at my apartment and I suggested we go out for breakfast. I ordered bacon; he requested steak. Later that afternoon, we stopped off for a late lunch at Burger King. I ordered a ham and cheese sandwich; he ordered beef without cheese. In my mind, as I projected how this could affect a potential marriage, I became somewhat agitated. "Why do you think you have to keep the dietary laws when you're not Jewish?"

A rather heated discussion followed. When we returned to my apartment, I asked that Bob leave immediately and return to Wichita. I remember as he loaded some items into his trunk, he turned to me and said, "I just realized that this may be the last time I ever see you."

"Oh, silly, no it won't!" I replied, although as upset as I was, I was wondering if it just might be.

Somehow, with all the bumpy discussions, I still knew Bob was finally "the one". After our very first date, I actually walked into my boss's office at Fidelity National Bank and announced, "Last night, I met the man I'm going to marry." Seven months later, the prophecy rang true when I walked down the aisle to wed Robert Paul Schiermeyer. My parents were overjoyed as they loved Bob immensely and were happy to see that I had finally found someone "mature" to date and marry.

In some ways, we seemed like such opposites and the first year of marriage seemed to emphasize the differences. I have to admit, our first year was not exactly smooth sailing. Bob was raised Catholic, I was raised Baptist, although Bob did convert to a Baptist before I met him. He was raised in Los Angeles, California. I was raised in small town Oklahoma. He had traveled world-wide. I never traveled. He came from a large family of 14 children. I had one brother. He liked excitement: flying airplanes, deep sea diving, parachute jumping. I liked the quiet farm life. But, as different as we were, I still was attracted to him and our marriage began an adventure that has provided more excitement than I could have ever imagined.

3

Nine months after we were married, Bob and I moved from Wichita, Kansas, to Gaithersburg, Maryland. Bob began medical school at the Uniformed Services Medical School in Bethesda. Eleven months later, our first son, Robbie, was born. He had dark eyes, dark hair and was beautiful. For the first time, I experienced what it's like to love a child, and somehow, had some inkling of how my parents must have cared for me.

While in medical school, Bob and I still attended church faithfully at the First Baptist Church in Gaithersburg. Bob taught a young married couples class. Because of Bob's Bible knowledge and love of teaching, the class grew quickly and the church continued to be a vital part of our lives.

Our next child, Michael, was born in April, 1988. He was healthy and gorgeous and I felt doubly-blessed. Shortly after his birth, in August, 1988, we were transferred with the military to San Antonio, Texas. Bob was given permission to complete his fourth year of medical school and following internship in Texas. We were excited about the move because it placed us much closer to my parents in Oklahoma.

Again, Bob was a Sunday School teacher for the young married couples class at Village Parkway Baptist Church. Our two sons were enrolled in the Mother's Day Out program at the church, and then when our oldest son reached age 5, he began kindergarten at the church's religious school. In 1991, while we were living in Texas, our third child, Stephen, was born -another son - another wonderful blessing.

While living in San Antonio we also became close friends with our neighbors across the street, Rob and Cathy Rossio. Little did I know how much their lives would eventually play into our lives. At the time, Rob was a non-observant Jew. His wife, Cathy, was a non-Jew, formerly raised in the Methodist church. They had three children, very similar to the ages of our children. In 1991, the Rossios were transferred from San Antonio to the Air Force Base in Dayton, Ohio. I remember thinking, "Who would want to go to Ohio?" But, they did have family there and I remember thinking how much I would miss them.

However, in 1993, my family, too, was transferred to Dayton, Ohio. Bob and I both found it particularly hard to move this time. We had close friends in Texas, were situated fairly close to my family in Oklahoma, liked our church, and liked the warm San Antonio climate. However, the Air Force mandated a move, and for the third time since we were married, we packed up and traveled to our new home in Enon, Ohio. (Enon is "none" spelled backward!)

Ohio was a pleasant surprise. The people were friendly, the climate was mild, the schools were good, and the Baptist church we joined was especially vibrant and exciting. They offered many Bible classes and we met many young military families, similar to us, in their congregation. We felt as though we fit right in, at least at first. And again, my husband's Bible knowledge became readily apparent during question and discussion periods in Sunday School class and he was soon invited to teach a class.

I was now 36 years old, well-established in my marriage with a family, but sensed a need to re-evaluate my life. More importantly than anything else, I began to feel that I wanted a much deeper relationship with God. As I mentioned earlier, I had attended church all my life and had tried to do all the things the church taught necessary for a fulfilled life: I had prayed at an early age for Jesus to be my Savior, (I had actually asked several times—just to make sure I got it right), been baptized, prayed daily, studied my Bible, and attended church regularly. However, it just seemed as though there was a need for something deeper. It wasn't that I felt depressed or unhappy. I couldn't really pinpoint what it was. I just thought it was probably that I needed more Bible study and prayer time. I reasoned the more I prayed and read my Bible, the closer I would come to God. I remember, before going to sleep one night, praying sincerely, "God, I REALLY want to know you—whatever the cost. Whatever it takes, please lead me into a deeper and more meaningful relationship with you." Little did I know what was to follow . . .

4

I reasoned that if I really wanted a deeper relationship with God, then I should study my Bible more seriously. I felt I should be willing to study with the full intent of doing what it said—even if no one else felt the teaching was relevant to them. One of the first verses that seemed to penetrate my mind, and would not go away, was in the New Testament, I Corinthians, where the Apostle Paul talked about women covering their heads. My first thought was, "Here we go again!" Bob and I had talked about this, in length, before we married. Apparently, in the Catholic Church where my husband grew up, women covered their heads when they prayed. He mentioned this practice to me when we were dating. He explained all the reasons why it made sense, to him, based on Scripture, for women to cover their heads.

In exasperation, I finally answered, "Well, I can tell you that because it is NOT practiced in the Baptist church, there must be a very good reason why. And I do NOT feel led to wear a hat, a doily, or anything else for that matter on my head! Also, I would appreciate it if you would stop bringing this up to me!"

Although I couldn't ever totally soothe my conscience as to why I didn't cover my head, I reassured myself that no one else in the church did it, and if they didn't do it, then surely why should I have to do it? However, I had now made a commitment to myself, that if the Bible said to do something, I would do it—unless someone could show me good reason otherwise. I talked with the pastor about head coverings. I ordered a tape on First Corinthians, by John McArthur, a well-known Christian pastor and radio personality. I read books about it. I talked with trusted friends. No one could really give me a good answer, other than "that was just for those times." Then, I would discuss it with my husband and he would answer, "If it was just for those times, then why, of all the million things God could have chosen to record in His Bible, He chose that?" I couldn't resolve that argument.

I kept thinking, "Okay, I've chosen to do whatever God asks me to do, and now I can't even get past this first thing." I remember one day in particular. I was emotionally distraught and waffling back and forth over what I should do because, for me, this represented more than just covering my head. It represented my willingness to do whatever God commanded. I remember crying and talking to my husband at the kitchen table.

"Why does this not bother anyone except me? Why is this such a big issue?"

I just can't quit thinking, "Do I really want to walk around, wearing a hat wherever I go? Would you be embarrassed if I came to the Emergency Room to visit you wearing a hat?" (Bob said it would be fine if I did.)

Suddenly, there was a light knock at the door. My neighbor and friend from church, Brenda, slightly opened the door with a smile. She quickly and embarrassingly retreated, "Oh! I can see this is a bad time. I'll come back later!" Then, she rushed away to her car.

I picked up the phone, a few minutes later, to talk with her.

"I know this is going to sound really funny, but I've really been struggling with a spiritual issue. I've been reading about head coverings, and for some reason, I can't seem to resolve it. I feel led to wear one, but at the same time, I'm embarrassed and don't know what to do."

Brenda, being very sympathetic and supportive answered, "Look, if you really feel that way, I've got a very pretty hat and I'll just give it to you. You can kinda try it out that way."

"Are you sure?" I asked in tears.

"Positive," she replied.

I took the hat and decided I could wear it to church. The problem was that no one wore a hat in our 300+ member church. I felt as though I couldn't have been more noticed if I were wearing a neon-flashing billboard. I felt as though people thought I was only trying to be stylish, albeit unusual, and noticed. Some people would comment on it; others would say nothing, but it was apparent that everyone knew me as "the hat lady". One evening, I remember sitting in the back of the church, trying to be discrete. The church was large enough to seat hundreds of people.. When heads were bowed for prayer, I quietly took out a scarf and placed it over my head. Immediately following the church service, one of my "friends", Sara, who had been seated in the front row of church, rushed quickly to the back of the church building, laughing hilariously with glee, for all to hear, "Marcella!!! I saw you sitting in the back with your SCARF when you prayed!" The issue of head coverings became very serious for me. I wanted desperately for someone else to also share my convictions, but unfortunately, no one did. There was a sense of frustration as I was trying to do the right thing, but kept wondering, if this was the right thing, then why did no one else feel that it was? However, I was determined that I had started on a path to become closer to God and if it meant doing things that didn't make sense to anyone else, so be it.

5

A few months later, the issue of head coverings took a backseat to a much larger, looming issue. It started when Bob attended a Continuing Medical Education Conference in San Antonio, Texas with Reuvain Rossio, (formerly Rob Rossio, our neighbor from San Antonio who had been transferred to Dayton, Ohio, a year before my family). Reuvain was also a doctor in the Air Force. During the two years the Rossio family had been in Dayton, they had made a dramatic move towards more observant Judaism. It was a topic of excitement for Reuvain and because my husband was always open to topics of religion, a very lively discussion ensued while on the flight back and forth from San Antonio. Reuvain had recently attended a lecture by Rabbi Tovia Singer. He was so impressed by his talk that he purchased a complete set of his tapes, entitled "Let's Get Biblical". Rabbi Singer's intent was to bring Jews back to their Biblical roots and strengthen their faith in Judaism. Reuvain invited my husband to listen to the tapes. Bob agreed, thinking that by listening to the tapes, not only would he find them interesting, but also a tool by which he could demonstrate the credibility of his own Christian faith and be able to explain to Reuvain why he still accepted Christianity as his own true faith.

The tapes were quite comprehensive and intense, to say the least. To my husband's surprise and dismay, he believed that the rabbi articulated Christian doctrine much better than many Christian pastors. Rabbi Singer raised many serious questions about the validity of the New Testament scriptures. He discussed, in detail, prophetic Christian scriptures and why Jews do not accept those scriptures. He talked about the written and oral Laws of Judaism and why Jews still view both of them as very important. He talked about many other serious concerns that Jews have with Christian doctrine.

After listening to the tapes, Bob commented to me that the rabbi had very valid points—to the point of being troubling to him. My response was "Who cares what he says? I'm sure the Jews have some contriving way to explain away why they can't believe in Jesus. They have to. Don't you see? They're blinded! They can't see Jesus as the messiah!"

My husband was steadfast, though, in seeking the truth. I quietly assured myself that this would all pass. I kept thinking, "Bob must not have the close relationship with Jesus that I do—or else this would not bother him. I'll just pray for him and soon, hopefully, all these questions he has will be resolved. He just needs to look a little closer at the Bible and he'll find the answers he needs."

In the meantime, I was a bit unsettled that Bob would even question Christianity. However, I was confident, that with time, things would become clearer.

Weeks passed and my husband seemed a bit different: pre-occupied and quiet. Something was going on—I knew that for sure. He was spending a tremendous amount of time in his office, reading and studying.

One Saturday morning remains forever etched in my memory. I was preparing to take our oldest son, Robbie, to the eye doctor, about a 25 minute drive into Springfield, Ohio. Before I left the house, I popped my head into Bob's office to say "good-bye." There he was again, intently listening to the "Let's Get Biblical" tapes. He literally couldn't put them down. As I pulled our van out of the garage, it was raining--a torrential downpour. All the sudden, it hit me: my husband is listening to these tapes because he actually may believe them! Talk about your life passing before your eyes! All I could think about was, "What if . . . Where does that leave me now? What if Bob would actually consider denouncing Christianity? No . . . he wouldn't do that . . . or WOULD he? Wow! What would I do if I wasn't married to a Christian man, or even worse, what if he wanted to be JEWISH?!" My husband is considering leaving the faith for what? For Jews?? The Jews were the ones who KILLED Jesus! The Jews were the ones who were never enlightened enough to realize that he was the true messiah! Although I had never really known too many Jews, growing up in Oklahoma, I didn't like the few I had known, except for the Rossios. Surely he didn't want to be like THEM! How would this affect our kids? What would my family say?" All of a sudden, tears began to flow as I drove down the winding country road towards Springfield. "How could this be happening to me?" Whether it was from my tears or the pounding rain, I could barely see. Not only could I not see the present road in front of me, I certainly couldn't see what lied in the road ahead for years to come. Thoughts of "What could happen if . . . and what would I do if . . . and what would my family do . . . " pelted my brain as I drove to the eye doctor.

6

When Robbie and I returned from the eye doctor's appointment, I sat in the van in the garage for several minutes, trying to regain composure before entering the house.

My son, Robbie, quietly asked, "Why are you crying?" I said, "Because ever since Daddy went on that trip with Mr. Rossio, he's been studying Jewish tapes and questioning all sorts of things about Christianity."

Robbie responded, "Oh, you mean you think he wants to be Jewish?" I answered back, "I don't know for sure. I just know this really bothers me."

Robbie quietly responded, "Oh, I guess that would bother me, too."

I finally walked silently into the house and into the kitchen to prepare lunch. In just a few minutes, Bob appeared. Trying to exercise restraint, but also feeling as though I wanted to explode, I asked Bob, "So why is it you're willing to listen to a rabbi?"

Bob replied, "Because truth is truth, no matter who presents it. I just want to know the truth." I was so bothered that Bob was even willing to give credibility to a RABBI, because after all, a rabbi was a leader of the Jews—the ones who killed Jesus. I put down my potato peeler, and with tears streaming down my face, yelled and protested, "How can you do this? What about your relationship with Jesus? What about all the experiences we've had because we're Christians?"

To my anger and dismay, Bob calmly commented to me that all religions, regardless of who they are, have "special experiences" because God loves everyone, regardless of their religion. He went on to say that ever since he had become a Christian that there were certain verses that he found troubling in the "New Testament." However, he had put them into a "faith pit", as advised him by a pastor, in hopes that he eventually would find answers to them. However, as he listened to the rabbi's tapes, he explained, all the dots began to suddenly connect and all the loose ends began to come together. His questions no longer seemed like questions, but answers. The rabbi's tapes actually made sense, and then he paused with a sigh, "So, I don't know what to do. I literally don't know what to do."

After some thought, I replied, "Call Vendyl Jones!" Vendyl Jones was a Baptist minister from Texas who we were familiar with because of his teaching tapes and his well-known excavations in Israel. In his lectures, he focused on Christian scriptures from a Jewish perspective. His stance was that in order to understand the "New Testament," one first had to understand the "Old Testament." I couldn't believe I was actually endorsing Vendyl Jones. When Bob and I were married, 10 years earlier, Bob had a set of his tapes that he would listen to frequently, especially while in the car. I cringed hearing his Southern twang and drawl (not that I don't have one myself, being from Oklahoma). He began every tape with a Southern drawl of "Shalom!" I remember asking Bob, "Does he have to say that every time?" Plus, I didn't understand why we had to learn everything Christian from a Jewish perspective. Vendyl did seem to know a lot about Judaism, and I figured if my husband wanted someone with a more Jewish background, Vendyl Jones would be the man. My husband said, "I can't just pick up the phone and call Vendyl Jones!" I asked, "Why not?" He thought telephoning someone such as Vendyl Jones was akin to trying to reach the Pope by phone. After much discussion, Bob picked up the phone and dialed, and to his amazing surprise, Vendyl Jones answered the phone.

"Hello, Vendyl?" my husband asked rather nervously. This is Bob Schiermeyer. How are you?" He went on to explain the dilemma he was in. I was standing close by, straining to listen, but with little success. Unbeknown to me, and after much study, Vendyl Jones was explaining to Bob that he no longer accepted the New Testament teachings as totally inerrant. This was something Bob did not think I was ready to hear, and as soon as Bob hung up the phone and I asked, "What did he say? What'd he say?" Bob was not very forthright in explaining exactly what Vendyl had said. He did reply that Vendyl explained that there were discrepancies in the birth narrative of the New Testament, but that the birth narrative was not in the original manuscripts. (I was thinking, "good, good, that explains that problem.") He went on to say that Vendyl believed that Jesus came for the Gentiles, not the Jews. This seemed like a rather radical concept, but one that would allow us to still cling to our faith, albeit a bit differently than other Christians. From other information my husband shared, Vendyl seemed to have reasonable explanations for at least some of the issues we were dealing with. I was hopeful, although guarded, that perhaps my husband, with further study and dialogue would come to the final resolution that Christianity actually still was true, as we had always believed, and life would continue as usual.

7

Almost immediately, at Vendyl Jones' recommendation, my husband began to study Hebrew in an effort to better understand Jewish scriptures. In addition, Vendyl was hosting a trip to Israel in a few months and wanted Bob to be part of the group. Bob had never been to Israel, but was anxious and willing to go. He thought, not only would it be a good opportunity to see Israel, but also an opportunity to have one-on-one dialogue with Vendyl Jones. Questions continued to arise over certain key texts in the New Testament and our conversations began to evolve, late into the night, over what we believed and why we believed it. We also began to look at verses in a way we had never looked at them before.

It was also at this time that Bob and I began to recall the irony of a book he had read just months earlier entitled, "A Skeleton in God's Closet". It was a fictional novel about an archeologist who had discovered Jesus' bones, thus disclaiming Jesus' resurrection. The book described the impact the discovery had on the whole community. As Bob and I discussed the book at that time we repeatedly remarked, "Wow! Can you imagine? Wouldn't that be horribly unimaginable?"

In the meantime, I suggested Bob arrange an appointment to meet with our pastor to discuss the questions and the concerns he was having. I said, "after all, he is our pastor and if this is troubling to our family, then we need to talk with him and seek his help. That's his job." So, at my bidding, Bob called the pastor and made an appointment to speak with him. As Bob began to outline some of his concerns to the pastor, Pastor Nicholson stopped him, "Bob, I don't have the answers for you. I just have faith that what I believe is true, and that's good enough for me." My husband left his office, thanking him for his time, but still without answers to some very troubling questions.

The same day my husband was meeting with the pastor at our church, I was meeting with teachers and children for Vacation Bible School. Every morning, for a week, approximately 150 area children would show up for summer Bible school. I had been asked to be a co-teacher for the first graders. Every morning, the Education director would welcome all the children, tell them how happy he was for them to be at church, and talk to them about Jesus. It was the church's goal to introduce many of the children, for the first time, to what it meant to be a Christian. It was also their goal to show them that the people of the church were different from the rest of the people of the world. They had something "special". Yet, one thing that bothered me intensely all week was that all the teachers dressed in jean shorts and tank tops to teach. One of the teachers actually sat with her legs straddled over the wooden railing, next to the podium, donning shorts and a halter top, while the assistant pastor spoke about Vacation Bible School.

I felt incredibly out of place and uncomfortable in that setting. I kept asking myself, "Why should I have to feel uncomfortable wearing a dress while in church?" Not only was I dealing secretly with my husband's struggle, but now I was angry that I should have to feel embarrassed about modesty. I was upset and angry that the church seemed to be setting a double standard. If the church was so "special", why were they trying to conform to the world, at least in dress? My anger and frustration peaked the day I took my first graders to music class in the sanctuary. The music teacher was preparing the kids for a musical presentation for the end of the week. On Sunday night, all the Vacation Bible school children were supposed to attend church with their parents and proudly show them what they had learned during the week. On this particular day, the music teacher was giving instructions as to when to arrive on Sunday evening, what to wear, etc. She then paused, looked straight at me, and in front of all the kids, said in a rather disgusted voice, "Do NOT wear a dress! I want you to look like everyone else." I felt myself becoming warm, my heart beating fast, the tears ebbing, and feeling like church was not the place it used to be.

After Vacation Bible School ended, the director of the school requested, the following week, that all the teachers complete a survey form on how the Bible school could be improved for the next year. I wrote several comments, questioning the issue of modesty in the school. To ensure my comments were not lost, I hand-delivered copies to the pastor, the assistant pastor, and the youth minister. Although I requested a response, no one replied.

8

As the weeks rolled on, so did my frustration over the whole "religion" situation. My husband, being a Sunday School teacher, and a very popular one - his class had grown from three married couples to over a dozen in less than a year - began to present his problems with the New Testament scriptures to his Sunday School class, such as problems with Jesus' genealogy, problems with prophetic scriptures, etc. His questions just happened to correlate with the week's assigned lesson for our class. Although my husband did not reveal his personal problems with the New Testament scriptures, members of the class were growing increasingly restless, wanting to know the answers to some of the questions.

I remember one young woman, Kim, in particular. She raised her hand one Sunday, and remarked, "Seriously, these are important questions! I want to know the answer!"

"Do your research" was the only comment Bob had.

I continued to wear my hat to church, feeling like probably no one understood the reason—that I was just a woman trying to make a poor attempt at being stylish and being noticed and also a bit weird.

After several weeks of Sunday school classes with a "Jewish bent", Bob received a telephone call from a rather prominent class member and church deacon, requesting a private meeting to discuss some serious concerns about the class. My husband agreed to meet at our home. The member encouraged my husband to resign as a teacher or else he threatened that he would go to the church board and demand his resignation. My husband agreed to resign. We continued to attend church and Sunday school class, but whenever my husband would raise his hand to ask a question or make a point, he was intentionally ignored. Bob and I both found it rather ironic that just a few months earlier, he had been approached by several key members of the class, asking if he would consider teaching a home Bible study class in addition to his Sunday class--because of his vast knowledge of the Bible and because everyone enjoyed his teaching so much!

I felt incredibly overwhelmed. I wanted to believe Christianity was true; I was scared to believe otherwise. On the other hand, my husband—who I knew to be very learned, was questioning core beliefs. What was wrong? Had he never really had a true, genuine spiritual experience? Was he not capable of faith? Why was it suddenly so hard for him to accept Christianity and so easy for him to accept Judaism? What was going on? I did a lot of crying during those days and a lot of soul-searching. I should also point out that, up to this point, I had neither listened to Rabbi Singer's tapes nor read his workbook. I had no interest in them. However, one day, while I was cleaning and dusting my husband's office, I picked up the "Let's Get Biblical" workbook and tapes. I thought to myself, "So, what IS the big deal? What could be so troubling to Bob?" I picked up the workbook that correlated with the tapes, just to peruse a few pages. I read about some of the prophetic passages Bob had been grappling with, and then turned to read some of the parallel comparisons of the New Testament gospels. There really were some rather glaring discrepancies that I had never seen before! I found this extremely troubling because in the church, I was taught that the New Testament was completely accurate—totally 100 percent. One very well-known Baptist minister had even been quoted as saying, "If you can find even one mistake, then the whole New Testament would have to be called into question." "What should I do with this?" I wondered. Then, I looked a bit further. I read the portion of the workbook that dealt with the oneness of God. I read verse after verse, "I, the Lord Your God am one. There is no other besides me." "God is not a man, nor the son of man (Who was Jesus referred to? The son of man.) There must have been at least 30 verses all pointing to the oneness of God—and, of course, nothing about Trinity (the three in one). I thought, "Well, this is certainly interesting, but after I talk to some very knowledgeable Christian pastor, all of this can be explained—I hope."

However, after noticing those few problems, more questions began to erupt in my mind. For example, "If Jesus was so crucial to man's salvation, why does God never mention his name in the Old Testament?" Or, "Why does He never say in the Old Testament, "I will send my son to die on a cross for you?" Or, "If Jesus is God, then how could the world survive when he died on a cross?" And, "If human sacrifice is forbidden under Jewish law, why would God choose that method to send His son to die?" And, "If the Law is forever, then why did Jesus have to die on the cross when the Law made provision for forgiveness of sin?" Or, "If God outlined in minute detail how the Law was to be carried out, why would he omit the one thing (Jesus) that was crucial to man's salvation?" One question led to another question and problems began to snowball. I wanted answers, but I didn't know who to ask.

9

The long-awaited month of November arrived, nine months after my husband had listened to the "Let's Get Biblical Tapes." I still was not emotionally ready to hear the tapes. I had only perused the surface of the workbook. My husband was prepared to travel on the much anticipated trip to Israel. And, he was going to meet with Vendyl Jones, who in my mind, was going to hopefully address many of my concerns. Bob was scheduled for learning, sight-seeing, and also some one-on-one learning with Vendyl Jones. I was bit apprehensive, but I prayed that the trip would bring answers and enlightenment to many of the questions we had been asking about Christianity. Usually, whenever someone traveled to Israel from our church, much attention and hoopla was given concerning the trip. The traveler was often requested to speak and even give a slide presentation upon his return. Before and after my husband's visit, no one from church said anything, not even "How was your trip, Bob?" The silence was deafening. No one wanted to hear about my husband's trip, before or after.

During Bob's absence, I did receive a phone call from Kim, a member of the Sunday School class, inviting me to her house for a Thanksgiving meal. I declined as I could already sense her tension around me. After extending the dinner invitation, she expressed her concern for my husband and me. I tried to explain to her, at least in part, what had prompted some of my questions. In tears, I told her that I didn't know the answers, but it would be encouraging if someone was, at least, willing to acknowledge that there were some issues that needed to be resolved. She responded, "I don't know, but that's where you just need to do more Bible study." I said, "Would you or your husband be willing to study some of these issues with us in an attempt to find answers?" Her response was "no, I don't think so."

Incredible frustration began to mount from this type of response—not just from Kim, but from anyone I tried to speak to from the church. Christianity—at least the Christianity I was taught—believes that Jesus is the only answer for man's sins. If man does not believe in Jesus, then he will burn alone, in a fiery hell of damnation—forever and forever. I could not understand how if someone truly believed this, why he or she would not be willing, at any cost, to research the Scriptures with me, and to probe and ask questions and invite discussion from learned ministers or pastors. Instead, the response was almost always the same: anger, ignorance, and silence.

I specifically remember the first Sunday upon Bob's return. The director of the Sunday School department asked if there were any prayer requests that morning. There were the usual requests, "Please pray for my sick sister." "Please pray that my job works out." "Please pray that we get the right military assignment." As people made their individual requests, people were nodding their heads in concern and understanding. Then, my husband raised his hand and said, "As you may have noticed by now, my wife and I have been struggling with some issues relating to New Testament scriptures and how they relate correctly with the Old Testament. We would really appreciate your prayers." Suddenly, it was as if the room froze in silence. Not a word was spoken, not a head nodded. Then, when the director led a prayer, audibly, for all the spoken requests, my husband's request for prayer was noticeably and painfully absent.

Immediately afterwards, the Sunday school department split into small groups for class and discussion. One of the members, whom I considered a close friend of Bob's, approached me with the most solemn expression, shoved me a book Bob had loaned him to read, and with anger and frustration in his voice quipped, "Here's Bob's book. Tell him I'm not interested in reading it." Class then commenced and I found myself holding back sobs through the entire class. I felt like we were suddenly losing most of our friends. I wasn't sure what I believed any more. My husband was slowly turning away from our traditional beliefs, I was feeling like I didn't know which way to go. Intense questions began to swell: Did I believe in Jesus the way I used to? Did I believe in the New Testament scriptures? Were they reliable? Were we really accepted in the church anymore? How much were people talking behind our backs?

I remember standing in front of our big upstairs bedroom window on a daily basis, looking towards the heavens and praying, "God, I don't want to offend you. If Jesus really is your son and you sent him to die for me, then I want to accept that, but if I've been deceived, please help me to know that, as well."

10

December arrived with much excitement—but not exactly with the Christmas magic I had anticipated. The previous year Bob and I had hosted the annual Sunday School Christmas party. By the numbers in attendance and the feedback we received later during the year, it appeared to be a well-received success. However, that year when the host and hostess became sick with the stomach virus, not to mention that the hostess was involved in a serious car accident only days before the event, when Bob and I offered to host, we were told we could not fill in to host the party. People were feeling pretty uncomfortable around us and, apparently, no one wanted to chance the topic of "religion" arising at the Christmas party. Since we could not host the party, we assumed we probably were not welcome in attendance either.

Approximately one week after the Christmas party, we received a phone call from Chris Williams, another prominent member of the Young Adult Sunday School class. He said that he would like to set up a meeting with Bob, along with four other members of the class. Bob and I excitedly agreed, thinking, "Someone is going to talk with us. We're finally going to get some of these issues out in the open!" I happily made preparations around the house for their visit. The tree was brightly lit and decorated that evening, the fireplace was crackling, and warm yummy brownies and spiced tea were awaiting our visitors on that fateful evening of December 12, 1994. We nervously awaited their arrival. At 7:30 pm, the doorbell rang. We rushed to answer the door, only to be greeted by five very somber-looking men. Bob extended a greeting for them to come in. The men managed to mumble a "hello", but other than that, they resembled a committee who had just been sent to deliver some very grievous news. They looked down at the floor. We invited them into the house to be seated at our kitchen table. Already feeling a bit tentative, I asked, "Would anyone like some brownies, some hot tea?"

Some of the men muttered, "no", the rest of group ignored me. Then, the "speaker" for the group started,

"Bob, we came here tonight to talk to you about your beliefs. Just who do you think Jesus is?"

Bob replied, "He's my lord and savior."

They then asked, "What do you think about the Trinity?" Bob replied, "I think it's idolatry."

They then asked, "So, with a belief like that, what are you doing as a member of our church?"

Bob said, "Well, I don't know. (pause) I guess I can resign."

Suddenly, the doorbell rang. It was Steve, the husband of the woman who loaned me the lace hat to wear to church. Steven was a good friend and when we told him about the meeting he said, he too, would like to attend.

He sat down at the table and said, "Well, I would just like to ask some questions."

The other men quizzically looked at him and asked, "What are you doing here? You weren't invited!"

He said, "Well, I thought perhaps I could come as a mediator."

The rest of the group snapped, "No one invited you as a MEDIATOR!"

Bob desperately wanted to discuss some of the issues he had been struggling with, in particular, the Trinity. As he began to quote scripture in an attempt to address at least one or two issues, Jim Ethridge, one of the committee members, held up his hand to him and said, "Bob, you know more scripture than we ever will. We can't discuss this with you. We just have faith and that's all we need."

I, gulping back the tears, asked "Could I just say one thing?"

The speaker for the committee said, "Go ahead."

"How would you feel if everything you believed in your whole life were suddenly being called into question and no one cared enough to talk about it —especially your friends from church, or your pastor? Would you not want someone to befriend you and help you find the truth? Would you not want someone to have enough compassion to help you?"

Chris, the leader, responded, "Marcella, I know there are many women in the church that think very highly of you—they really do. I'm really sorry for this. I really am." Then, with that, the group said, "Well I guess there's not much more to say." They, then, somberly stood up from their chairs and walked quickly to the door. The much anticipated meeting was over. The men were gone; we were officially out of the church.

I sat on the couch, in front of the quiet twinkling Christmas lights, tears streaming down my cheeks. Where would we go from here? What would my parents think—if they even knew? Who would be our friends? What would we tell our kids? What was true? Who would show us the truth—or even yet —who would even be willing to discuss the scriptures with us?

Bob lingered at the door to say "good bye" to Steve, the neighbor who attempted to be the mediator. I remember Steve saying to me, "It's not the end of the world, Marcella." (easy for him to say). He then left and Bob walked over to me and asked, "What do you want to do now?"

I remember saying, "Well, I guess we can find another church and just keep our mouths shut about what has happened. Don't tell anyone that our beliefs are different than theirs."

11

The next few weeks were very difficult ones. In fact, the very next morning, when my neighbor across the street called to talk, I burst into tears. My son, Michael, then 7 years old, had answered the phone. He had stayed home from school that day because of a cold. When he handed the phone to me, my neighbor, Kathy, asked "What's wrong with Michael?" I burst into uncontrollable sobs and answered, "He has a cold." There was silence . . . . then she replied, "surely that's not all that's wrong?" Yes, she was right . . . that was not all that was wrong. My whole life seemed to be hanging in the balance. Everything I had based my life on was being called into question. Where would I go from here? Kathy invited me to go to lunch and do some light shopping. She suggested that it would help "take my mind off of things." I do like lunch and shopping, but nothing was going to take my mind off of this. I remember going with her and feeling as though I was in a daze, both from crying and despair and having this horrible, sinking feeling that things were going to get a lot worse before they ever got better.

As the days and weeks passed, my concern over what was going to happen became an all-consuming thought. I wanted so desperately to share my plight with someone —but with whom? My parents would be devastated, my friends from church were afraid of me, and casual friends could not understand the heaviness of the situation. I did a lot of praying and a lot of crying. I also listened to music. Because almost all of our music was Christian music and I noticed that my husband didn't want to listen to songs about Jesus anymore, I would select songs that only mentioned God's name. There was one in particular that had the lyrics of "God is too wise to be mistaken; God is too good to be cruel." Somehow, I found those words very comforting and would listen to them over and over again. There was another song about King David and how that "When others see a shepherd boy, God may see a king." It, too, was a very beautiful song and would encourage me that perhaps things were not always as they seemed.

Fortunately, we didn't have to make an immediate decision about where to attend church because every weekend, for about a month, Dayton received huge snowfall amounts and area churches cancelled their services. However, we finally had a Sunday in which the weather was pleasant and we made a trip to the closest Baptist church in town: Enon First Baptist Church. It was very small, maybe 50-75 members, but people were very warm and welcoming, and they had a small youth group for my boys. It was a bit uncomfortable, though, when members would greet us with "Oh, are you new in town?" We would simply reply, "No, we just never saw your church before—it was so hidden away in this town!" We started attending the church weekly, but things seemed different. My husband seemed a bit detached from the services, I seemed to be holding my breath that the pastor didn't mention Jesus' name too often and offend my husband, and the kids seemed to be trying really hard to be excited about the youth program.

We attended services for a few weeks until one fateful Sunday in February, approximately one year from the time Bob had made the trip with Mr. Rossio. Bob and I walked into church services one morning, sat down, but within a few minutes, Bob mentioned that his back was hurting so much (he suffers chronic back pain from two surgeries) that he needed to step outside the building and be able to stand up rather than sit. I sat through the remainder of the service with the boys then met Bob outside in the van. As we slowly drove towards our house, Bob commented, "I saw something this morning that I've never seen before." He asked me to open up to the book of Leviticus and read Chapter 6 verse 26. He then said, "Do you realize what that's saying?" (I didn't.) He then went on to explain that the verse taught that any sin offering (Jesus was supposed to be the ultimate sin offering) whose blood was taken in and sprinkled in the holiest place (Jesus' blood was allegedly sprinkled in the heavenly holy of holies) had to be taken outside the camp and totally burned. It could not be eaten; it had to be cremated. So, he went on to ask, "why does Christianity either literally or symbolically eat and drink Jesus' body and blood? Besides, Jesus wasn't cremated. And the Bible teaches that we aren't supposed to consume blood." We drove quietly home, but as we walked into the house, Bob put his Bible down, then looked at me and said, "I'm never going back."

12

Hearing the news that my husband was "never going back" was like hearing the news that a dear friend had died after a long and debilitating illness. I was sad, a bit numb, but not totally surprised. All I could think about were the ramifications of such a decision. What now? How would I tell my parents? What would happen to our family? How would we continue to learn if we were not in the church? Would we teach ourselves for the rest of our lives? How would we know the truth? Who would be our friends? How would our children be affected?

The next few months were a very dark time in my life. I spent many hours crying and agonizing over what would be. I was scared about the decision we had made to leave the church: how it would affect not only me, but my children, my husband, my parents, my circle of friends. Had we made the right decision? If we were wrong, the ramifications were enormous. I felt such an overwhelming cloud of despair that I must confess that I wished to die more than live. I kept thinking of the pain and hurt, not to mention shock, that would affect my parents. I thought about my children and the confusion they would have to endure over our experience. I thought about my husband and how he would be perceived by friends and co-workers. I would go to the bathroom, numerous times during the day, just to cry, so that my children and husband would not see me crying in front of them. In despair and depression, I prayed to die numerous times. It is shamefully painful for me now to admit it, but at the time, I felt it would be better to die than to face the challenging road ahead. I felt my husband could possibly handle it; I could not.

I attempted to find help by writing a letter to a very well-known and popular Baptist minister in Atlanta, Georgia. He had authored many best-selling books, hosted a very successful TV ministry, and was the pastor of a very large and thriving church in Atlanta. Although I admit he probably receives hundreds of letters a day, I was hoping mine would be different enough to elicit a response. I explained my situation, mailed him a copy of my husband's book, and requested help in finding answers to some of the serious questions that had arisen in our lives. I waited for many weeks, only to receive a short letter from his office, explaining that an unsuccessful attempt had been made to contact me by phone. The letter went on to state that because I could not be contacted personally, (no message was ever left on the phone), they would be unable to help me because of confidentiality risks.

The next few months proved to be most challenging. We held our own "church services" in our home, trying to sing familiar songs with the kids and then read and discuss passages from the Bible. We did share with Robbie, Michael, and Stephen some of the most troubling New Testament verses that had eventually led us away from the church.

"Do you understand why we might have had a problem with these verses?" Robbie, our oldest, then 10 years old, responded, "Well, yeah!" as though he was surprised we had not seen those verses before. Our other two boys could not understood exactly what was transpiring, but they were still willing to learn with us at home as a family. Although we were trying to make the best of the situation, the whole family was acutely aware that things were different—very different. When we read passages from the Tanach ("Old Testament"), I would get upset with Bob when he was pronouncing all the names differently from what I had heard. He explained that he was trying to pronounce them as they would be pronounced in the Hebrew language since they were Hebrew characters. To me, it just seemed as though one more thing had changed and I didn't like the change. I knew we were seeking the truth, but somehow, seeking the truth was not as easy as I had hoped. I felt lonely and isolated, my kids were feeling uncomfortable at a private Christian school, and resentment towards my husband was slowing brewing.

13

In February, 1996, one year after my husband had traveled with Ruvain and received the tapes, I received the news that I needed surgery to remove a bladder tumor. This was to be my third surgery within the past nine months. While everything else was swirling in the religious world the previous year, I had also been diagnosed with bladder tumors during the year, one in April, another in October, and now, another one in February. Although the doctor told me it was not cancer, I could not stop worrying about what was causing the tumors. Was there a connection between my prayers in the bathroom to die and the fact that I was experiencing bladder problems?

I remember one Sunday in particular. After many hours of preparation, I served a large Sunday meal of turkey, dressing, and all the trimmings. Although we no longer attended church, Sunday dinner was a tradition in our family—one I wanted to continue to embrace. As we were sitting at the table, Bob asked, "Do the potatoes have butter in them?" (According to the Jewish dietary laws he had been studying, Jews do not mix meat and dairy products.) I replied, "yes". He said, "Oh, then I guess I won't have any." He then went to help himself to the corn and I said, "Well, the corn has butter in it, too."

"Oh", he said quietly.

Bob hardly touched the food, and besides being annoyed that I had spent hours preparing a meal that he would not eat, I began to realize that almost everything I had cooked had some type of either milk or butter in it. I then began to think, "Wow—does this mean we can't even celebrate Thanksgiving ever again? Because I certainly have no idea how I would make gravy or potatoes or vegetables without butter and milk." I then began to think that here was one more tradition we would have to give up because of "our change". I began to cry at the table. My crying soon turned into anger: anger at my husband, anger at the thought of having to change the way I cook, anger at not being able to go to church, and anger at having to have surgery the following week. I stood up from the table and in between sobs and tears, I cried, "Maybe if you're lucky, I'll die next week in surgery, and then you won't have to deal with me anymore! You can cook the way you want to cook, eat the foods you want to eat, and raise your kids the way you want to raise them. I won't be in the way anymore!"

My husband calmly replied, "Why are you angry at me just because I want to be more spiritual in the way I eat my food?"

"It would be one thing if you told me beforehand, but to let me spend hours slaving in the kitchen to serve a meal and then announce that you're not going to eat it—especially when you're not Jewish—is pretty inconsiderate! Oh, and just for your information, I don't want to be Jewish! I don't want to be Jewish! I don't want to be Jewish!" I screamed at the top of my lungs. I then grabbed my purse and left. I had to get out of there and go somewhere. I didn't know where—but somewhere—alone—to think.

I drove to the Enon City Park. I pulled alongside the road and stopped the car. The park was small and quiet, not too many people, and was peaceful. I sat for a very long time: thinking, crying, and praying. After an hour or more, I finally came to the conclusion that the problems were not going away. Life would go on; I would have to deal with them one by one, day by day, and that I would survive. I turned the car around and headed home.

Still feeling as though my existence had been eaten and swallowed alive, I returned home to find my children playing and my husband reading. I sat down on the couch to read to Michael, my eight- year- old. Swallowing hard to maintain my composure, I began to read to him. After a few minutes, the phone rang. "Yes, how are you?" I could hear Bob saying. "Oh, yes! She's here." I was agonizing, "please don't call me—PLEASE don't call me to the phone." But, it was too late. Bob had already told my father I was home and summoned me to the phone.

I had not yet shared with my parents the painful dilemma I was experiencing. However, this afternoon, I had no choice.

"Marcella? How are you?" my father asked, in his usual tone.

"Fine" I replied, swallowing hard.

"What were you doing?"

"Reading Michael a book", as my voice began to quiver and tears begin to swell.

"What's wrong?"

"I don't know," I lied.

"Do you want to speak with your mother?"

"Okay."

My mother was summoned to the phone and I slowly spilled the story of how Bob had been participating in some special Bible studies and how some serious questions had evolved about our original beliefs in Christianity. In tears, I explained how we had left the church, were searching for answers, and how I was having a difficult time coping.

My mother, in her maternal soothing voice, assured me that she would help me. She explained that there was a pastor currently visiting her church who was very learned and who would be "just the man" to examine our questions and help us sort through our haunting questions. I revealed to my mother that Bob had written a short "book", in an effort to put his thoughts to paper, on many of the discrepancies and problems we were facing with Christianity. My mother offered to take the book to the pastor for his perusal and feedback. I thanked my mother, feeling a bit embarrassed and emotionally drained, said, "thank you", "bye", and hung up, with a ray of hope. The "cat was out of the bag". Now, what would happen?

Bob packaged his "book" the next week and mailed it to my mom. Weeks passed and while curiosity was tormenting me, I said nothing. Although I spoke with my parents weekly, mentioning the religion issue was very difficult —so difficult I couldn't discuss it. They also said nothing.

Finally, after several weeks, one Wednesday evening, my mother telephoned to talk. As my heart pounded from fear, I hesitantly asked, "Did your pastor have a chance to look at Bob's book?"

There was a long pause, a sigh, and then my mother said, "Marcella, I can only tell you what he told me. He said 'this book was written by a very angry man. I can't respond to someone like this. That's not how our religion works.'"

"But Mom, what are we supposed to do then?" I cried in desperation!

"Well, Marcella, I just don't see what your questions are. I've looked at them and honestly cannot see what the problem is."

"Could we take the book and go over some of the questions that I have over the phone?"

"No, I don't think that would be necessary."

"Mom!" Screaming through tears and more disrespectfully than I want to admit, "There's no one out there who wants to talk to us! Please don't just ignore us! I need help! I want to believe like you, but first, I need to discuss some of these problems. How am I supposed to resolve them, if no one is willing to talk to me?"

We argued back and forth, my mom insisting that there were no problems and I insisting that there were. As we were talking, I heard the door open on the other end, and my father returning from the usual Wednesday evening church service. "I've got to go, Marcella." My mom hurriedly whispered. The conversation ended.

14

As it is with life, there is usually not just one challenge to face, but several. While I was struggling with the religion issue, I was also becoming increasingly apprehensive about my family's upcoming move to, unbelievably, Oklahoma. Ever since I married and joined my husband to be an Air Force wife, we had moved several times. I always bemoaned the fact that my parents were hundreds of miles apart from me. First, I moved from Oklahoma to Kansas, then Maryland, then Texas, and then Ohio. I would often fantasize how wonderful it would be to have my parents close by to visit with, to share meals with, and to have babysitting—especially when I was sick or just needed a night out with my husband. I was always a bit jealous of those mothers who had their mom close by to help them. But now, after ten years of marriage, my husband was finally being transferred to Tinker AFB in Oklahoma City. Wow! Only an approximate one hour drive to my parent's house! I could finally be close to my parents. Or, could I? By this time, they knew that my family was no longer attending church. Our relationship was tense, at best. My parents were trying to be good parents by not interfering, but at the same time, they were deeply concerned for our salvation, especially the children. They feared if things didn't turn around quickly, then the family, including our precious children, were doomed to hell forever and ever. But, if I thought the relationship couldn't get any worse, I was painfully wrong.

My family made the move to Oklahoma in August, 1996. As my parents attempted to display excitement over my move, the tension and hurt between us was painfully obvious. It started the first day that the moving truck arrived. My parents arrived early to help unload and organize, but the truck was late (the driver eventually ended up in the hospital with diverticulitis), and my parents were visibly annoyed with the unexpected delay. Then, I could do nothing right. As my mother attempted to help me organize the new kitchen, she was upset with the contact paper I had chosen to line the kitchen shelves as it was too sticky, the movers were slow with unloading the clothes—which my parents had offered to unpack—and my kids were not eating enough of the food that my mother had prepared for them that day. Although all these things would normally be only minor inconveniences, because of the tension, it didn't take much to make things worse.

After settling into our new house, it was only a couple of weeks until school started. My two older boys had previously been enrolled in a private Christian school. Now, since that was no longer an option, all three boys, the youngest was to be in kindergarten, were to be enrolled in the local public school. After only two days of school, all three boys begged to be home schooled. I had to admit, the public school environment was not what I had hoped for: lack of respect for teachers and others in authority, no dress code (from which they could have desperately benefited), and curriculum that left much to be desired. Also, I was trying to compare the public school with the previous private school and I was not impressed. So, after much deliberation, I chose to home school all three children. I had a set curriculum and schedule and home schooling commenced shortly after removing them from the public school. One big problem, though: my parents had always been adamantly opposed to home schooling. Now, here was their daughter, choosing that option, which in itself would have been a big disappointment, but coupled with the religion issue, was a bombshell. I entertained the idea of NEVER telling them I was home schooling. But, it soon became apparent that was not a good idea. My mom began to ask questions concerning school and there was the possibility that my parents might just drop by the house some time—how would I explain the presence of all three boys at home during the day? I didn't have the courage to tell my parents face to face, so I sat down to write them a letter. I waited a couple of days after mailing the letter, and after not hearing anything from my parents, decided to give them a phone call to discuss what I had done.

"Hello, Daddy?"

"Yes."

"Did you get my letter?" I tentatively asked.

"Yes, we did. (long pause). Marcella, just what was it that caused you to leave the church?"

Shaking with emotion and nervousness, I responded, "Well, Bob and I had done a lot of study and we came to the conclusion that there were a lot of things in the church that were actually contrary to what the Bible teaches. Because no one was willing to discuss those issues or confront them, we decided we could no longer be comfortable in the church and it was time to do some study on our own."

"Issues like what?" my father responded.

"Well, like the Trinity, the issue of sin and atonement, and the accuracy of the New Testament."

"Marcella, you know the New Testament is true, always has been. What would make you change your mind, say for example, about the Trinity?"

In the meantime, the receiver on the other line clicked as my mother also picked up the phone. I recited some verses which seemed problematic to me and asked them what they thought.

"Marcella, you're not even trying to understand!" they responded in anger and frustration.

Perhaps they perceived that I wasn't, but in reality, I wanted nothing more than to understand! In desperation, I wanted someone to reach out to me and admit that there were some verses in the New Testament that were not making sense and even though these were verses we had based our lives upon, it was time to re-examine them—either to confirm our beliefs even more strongly or to admit there was a problem. Of course, there was a major difference between my parents' situation and mine. My parents had each other for support, plus their relatives, plus their entire church community, encouraging them that they were right in their beliefs. They believed I was wrong, my husband was evil, and that if they prayed enough for us, we would come back to our senses.

I, on the other hand, was married to someone who strongly believed that there was a problem with the New Testament scriptures, who had studied intensely, and was wanting to come to the truth—no matter what the cost. Of course, I had the option of saying I wanted nothing more to do with his approach to studying, that I would divorce him, and live my life back in the church, pleasing my family and friends. The only thing was . . . I knew deep inside there was a problem, as well. I could not, in good conscience, dismiss what we were learning because there was a problem—even though many people refused to see it or wanted to even consider the possibility. I had a lot more at risk than they did, one might say.

15

Up until this point, I had only studied Rabbi Singer's workbook on "Let's Get Biblical." However, there were several tapes in his tape workbook, covering a variety of topics from "Why Jews Don't Accept Jesus as the Messiah" to "The Trinity". It was finally time to sit down and listen to all the tapes, as my husband had done. It was an emotionally difficult task, but it was important. So, each evening, I would sit down with my husband at the kitchen table and intently listen to each tape. The facts were there—but they were hard to accept. So many things I had been taught as being "Biblical" were being called into question, and sadly enough for me, Rabbi Singer was able to support his teaching on scripture. I thought, "How could ANYONE listen to these tapes and still remain a Christian?!" There was still something deep inside, though, that ached to remain the way I was. I wanted to maintain the relationship I once had with my family and church friends, yet the information Rabbi Singer was giving over was irrefutable. I entertained the thought that perhaps Rabbi Singer was somehow craftily twisting scripture in such a way that I was being misled and that if perhaps I could find the right Christian theologian, he could unravel this mystery.

Then, Pastor Ralph Franklin entered. He was the associate pastor of the Southern Baptist Church in Del City, located only three miles from our current home. The main pastor of the church was Pastor Bailey Smith who had also served as past president of the national Southern Baptist Convention. Pastor Smith gained much attention in earlier years, while president of the SBC for his controversial statement that "God does not hear the prayer of the Jew." The current mission statement for the church this year was to "evangelize the Jew." After hearing of their mission, I told Bob that we should arrange a meeting with either the pastor or associate pastor at the church and discuss with them why Jews don't believe in Jesus. We should offer a set of Rabbi Singer's tapes and ask for help in deciphering where the rabbi had been misleading, thus leading us back to "the truth" and helping the church at the same time understand more about Judaism.

I called the church office the following week and talked with the church secretary. I explained briefly how my husband and I had been struggling with some difficult issues and needed help. She cheerily answered that "Ralph Franklin would be just the one you need to talk with!" She set up an appointment for me, my husband, along with my three boys, to meet with Pastor Franklin. The first meeting was very cordial. Pastor Franklin spoke comfortably with us and assured us that he would be happy to peruse Rabbi Singer's tapes. Before Bob and I left his office, we had already arranged another meeting for the following week to discuss the content of Rabbi Singer's tapes. I left feeling a bit doubtful, but at the same time, somewhat encouraged.

The following week, I began to rehearse in my mind the questions I wanted to ask Pastor Franklin after hearing his response to Rabbi Singer's tapes. Sadly, those questions never materialized. When we walked into Pastor Franklin's office that day, the mood was considerably different. We sat down and after just a few seconds, he reprimanded my husband for speaking to a technician at the Emergency Room where he worked about the "religion subject".

"I specifically asked you NOT to discuss this with ANYONE," Pastor Franklin stated somberly.

Apparently, a member of Pastor Franklin's church also happened to be a technician at the hospital where Bob was employed. He overheard Bob talking during the week, in confidence, to another doctor about Rabbi Singer's tapes. He interjected himself into the conversation, offering himself as very learned in apologetics. After much persistence, Bob relented and gave him a copy of the tapes. Unbeknownst to Bob, this technician and his wife were members of Pastor Franklin's congregation. The tapes, unfortunately, prompted a phone call from the technician's wife, in tears and hysteria, to Pastor Franklin. (Talk about timing.)

Thus, Pastor Franklin was upset with my husband and accused him of trying to break up Scott's marriage. My husband replied with the following scenario:

"I understand that you're upset. But, if you were sitting in an airport and talking to a Mormon about your Baptist beliefs, would you consider that as breaking up someone's marriage?"

It was obvious Pastor Franklin was upset and trying to control his aggravation. It was also obvious he had not listened to the tapes by Rabbi Singer. He dismissed us after only a few minutes, never to be heard from again.

16

Just a few short weeks later, my mother commented that there was a young gentleman in the church preparing a report on religion and that he had asked for more information on Judaism. Apparently, my parents had told him about me. He acknowledged that he knew very little, but would like to know more. I offered Rabbi Singer's tapes for both my parents and their friend. On my next visit to my parent's home, I asked my mother if she would be willing to listen to at least one of Rabbi Singer's tapes so that she could better understand some of the questions I was grappling with. She agreed. She brought a tape player to the kitchen table that evening and we both sat down to listen. Soon, my father was drawn to the table as well. After approximately ten minutes, my mother asked that the tape player be turned off.

"You don't want to listen to it anymore?" I asked.

"No, I don't," replied my mother. "I hate that tape and I hate that rabbi and I hate what he has done to you, Marcella. He has destroyed your faith and that's a terrible thing to do to anyone!"

My father stood up from the table and asked, "Marcella, what are you going to do when you are called to stand before the Judgment seat and asked, 'what did you do with my son?'"

I would reply, "In your Word, You said there is no other God and Savior besides You, and so I believed in You and You alone."

My father replied, "So you don't believe in Jesus anymore? What about the Trinity?"

"I want to, but there are so many verses that seem to imply otherwise," I cried.

As our voices began to rise with emotion, we stopped abruptly. My 12 year old son, Robbie, was in the bathroom, violently throwing up. Suddenly, we all felt sick to our stomachs.

17

I gradually and seriously began to conclude that no one was going to be able, as a Christian, to refute the discrepancies Rabbi Singer was presenting. Not my parents, not well-known pastors or lay leaders, not friends--no one. And, deep inside I had began to experience a feeling of resignation to Christianity.

One interesting sideline: While living in Oklahoma City, Bob and I decided we wanted to try to eat more kosher food. After making some telephone calls, I was informed that there was only one grocery store in Oklahoma City that carried kosher food, Puckett's, located on Portland Avenue. Turns out, the grocery store was within blocks of where I had lived over ten years ago. Not only that, right across the street was a Burger King, the same restaurant Bob and I visited when we were dating and suffered the steamy argument over Jewish dietary laws. Now, ten years later, we were returning as a family, with three kids, to buy kosher food at the kosher grocery store—directly across the street. In addition, while at the store one evening, the gentleman who stocked the shelves, Jerry Friedman, introduced himself to us. He explained that he was one of the few observant Jews living in Oklahoma City and how he had undertaken the job of stocking kosher food to help the Jewish community. He was a kind gentleman and he and his wife continued to stay in touch with us since our first encounter in the grocery store.

While living in Oklahoma City, my parents visited us for only one family meal, on my father's birthday. That was the last time they would ever join us for a home-cooked meal. There were many other invitations extended, but all were declined. It was obvious they felt incredibly uncomfortable in my home. From time to time, they would make unannounced visits, but they would visit only for a brief period, usually less than an hour, then excuse themselves to go home. All the while, we tried to ignore the bigger issue looming in front of us.

18

In addition to the religion issue, I was trying to cope with the issue of cancer. Although I had been told earlier, after three surgeries, that my bladder tumors were not cancer, once I moved to Oklahoma City, I was diagnosed with more tumors. Unfortunately, this time, the doctor told me they were cancer and recommended chemotherapy as treatment. I took a short round of chemotherapy for approximately three months. My first checkup was clear—but for the next checkup, three months later, I was not so fortunate. There was a small tumor, and in addition to that, there was one other minor complication—I was pregnant.

The pregnancy was a surprise, at 40 years of age. My urologist told me that while he would normally remove the bladder tumor immediately, he was advised by the OB doctor not to perform any procedure until after the first trimester for the health of the baby. So, I waited and worried.

At 12 weeks of pregnancy, I went for my first prenatal visit. The nurse was kind and relaxed and told me everything looked "normal". That was comforting to hear, especially after hearing so many abnormal reports concerning the bladder tumors. She also told me that she could hear the heartbeat at 185 beats per minute. When I returned home that day, I excitedly shared the news with my husband that everything was normal and that she even heard the heartbeat at 185 beats per minute! My husband paused for a moment, and then he said, "That's fast for one baby. I wonder if there were two and she was hearing the second heartbeat, as well."

"Oh, I don't think so . . . . I can't imagine having TWINS! Besides, don't you think the nurse would have detected them if that were the case?" I asked.

"Nevertheless, I should have you come out to the ER this evening and I could just do a quick ultrasound to check."

"I don't think that's necessary. Come on—you really think I have TWINS??"

Well, the more I thought about it, the more I decided perhaps I should take a quick trip to the ER, just to squelch any thought that there might be more than one baby. So, I loaded up all three of my boys: Stephen, Michael, and Robbie, and we headed to the ER for a quick peak.

The ER was quiet that evening, so the nurse ushered us to the ultrasound room with my husband. He smoothed the cold, squishy ultrasound jelly on my belly, then placed the monitor on me to have a look. Within seconds, my husband announced, "There they are—both of them! See--there they are!"

Robbie, Michael and Stephen reacted excitedly. "What? There's two babies!!" Then, Stephen remarked, calculatingly, "Mommy, that means you'll have to cook seven hamburgers instead of five!"

Excitement reigned supreme that evening. All I could think about was I was having twins. Wow! I always thought that happened to other people, not me. I called a couple of close friends to share the news. Not only had God chosen to bless us with another baby, but two! (Who knows? One might even be a girl this time!)

A few weeks thereafter, I was labeled a high-risk pregnancy and sent off-base for treatment at Dr. Chast's office, a doctor who specialized in high- risk pregnancies. During my first visit, Dr. Chast was very kind, but tried to explain to me the many risks involved with the pregnancy because of my age and because of the pre-existing cancer. I also remember him scanning my chart and remarking, "I see you're Jewish?" I replied, "Yes". (I knew I wasn't Jewish, but didn't know what else to put down.) He went on to explain the higher risk of Tay Sachs disease in Jews. I stammered, Well, I'm not really Jewish, well actually, it's a long story. I used to be a Christian, but now, my husband and I are thinking about being Jewish, and we've been studying." My voice trailed as I realized the doctor was really not interested in all the details. I just was not prepared for the topic to even arise.

I returned home that day, distraught and uneasy about the pregnancy: all the possible complications, everything from Down syndrome to a premature baby. Would I be able to carry this pregnancy to full-term, and if I did, would the babies be healthy? Also, what about the small tumor the urologist had found when I was only 6 weeks pregnant? What would I do about that?

Should I have the surgery to remove the tumor? The urologist said, "yes". The OB doctor said "no".

And one other thing, at some point in time, I was going to have to tell my parents that I was expecting twins. Because they had such strong beliefs about the destiny of anyone who does not believe in Jesus, (they are forever doomed to hell), how could I break the news to them that I was having more children?

I knew I couldn't hide the news forever, especially with two little babies growing in my tummy. So, one evening at about 15 weeks, I swallowed hard and picked up the telephone to call my mom and break the news.

The telephone rang . . . . "Hello?"

"Hello, Mother?" my voice quavering.

"Yes."

"What were you doing?"

"Oh, I was just outside getting some chores done."

"Well, I have some news for you. Are you sitting down?"

"Oh, I think I'm okay standing, thank you."

"Well, I'm pregnant again (silent pause) with twins."

"Oh! That'll be fun!" as she tried to sound excited, although I could sense the worry and shock in her voice.

"Would you be willing to help me with them the first week they're born?"

"Ohhhh no, oh no, you're on your own there! You'll have to take care of them yourself!"

"Okay", I whimpered, partly scared and partly hurt by the response. "I just wanted to let you know." Not knowing what else to say, I half whispered, " I guess I'll let you go."

"Okay, good bye."

"Bye."

19

As the weeks passed, depression set in as I worried about my life. There were no close friends from church, no one from a synagogue, and my family was uncomfortable being around me. I wanted to call my OB doctor to receive help for the depression, but was too scared and embarrassed. I was growing increasingly bigger by the day, I opted not to have bladder surgery in the interest of the pregnancy, and I desperately wanted someone close to talk to. I used to stand privately every morning, in front of the bathroom window (at that time, I didn't know it was inappropriate for Jews to pray in the bathroom), and ask God to protect my babies, to make them healthy and beautiful, and let me live.

However, there were many difficult days when I could not understand WHY we had to leave the church, WHY I had to have cancer, and WHY I was having babies at age 40! About the only friends I had were the moms on my son Stephen's baseball team. I also had one other very dear, close friend, Linda, whom I had known since first grade. She provided a tremendous amount of support for me. She lived in Tulsa, approximately an hour and a half away, and she would make regular trips to visit and help me.

On January 13, 1998, my OB doctor informed me that it was safe to deliver the twins (they were now 36 weeks by ultrasound). He asked if I would prefer Friday, January 16, or the following Monday. As uncomfortable as I was, (I had been measuring 40 weeks for a regular pregnancy at 28 weeks), I opted for Friday, January 16. At 8:00 am, the whole family arose early for the special day and we drove to the hospital. At 12:04 pm, Danielle Marie weighed in at 6 lbs. 7 ½ ozs. And 21 inches long. At 12:40 pm, Dakota Allen weighed in at the same weight and height as his sister. Two beautiful, healthy babies were given to my husband and me. Danielle was wrapped in pink, Dakota in blue. My husband carried them from the OR to the hospital room for each of the boys to see. Dakota was having some minor problems with breathing, so was taken to the nursery, but Danielle remained by my bedside. By Sunday, Danielle and I were able to return home. On Monday, Dakota came home—both healthy babies. I knew God had heard my prayers.

That same Monday evening, my good friend, Linda, came from Tulsa to stay with me and help out for the week. Although Linda considers herself a Christian, she never let that interfere with our friendship. She immediately stepped in to help care for the babies so that I could get some much needed rest. She took me clothes shopping for the twins, cooked all the meals, did housecleaning, and did a wonderful job of being a sensitive friend. We sat and talked for hours that week, holding the babies, reminiscing, but also talking about dreams for our present lives.

My parents were painfully absent that first week. However, my brother, my only sibling, did phone me on Saturday, a week after the twins were born to inquire how I was doing. I invited him to visit, and to my surprise, he caught a flight that same day from Houston to Oklahoma City, to come see his new little niece and nephew. He, too, was having difficulty coping with my doubts and rejection of traditional Christian beliefs. At one point during my pregnancy, he cut off all correspondence with me because he could no longer consider me his sister. He placed my name on his E-mail rejection list and requested that I not contact him. Just weeks before the twins were born, he called me to apologize and admitted that as a result of intense counseling, he wanted to re-establish a relationship. I was happy we were on speaking terms again.

Also, as a result of his visit that weekend, my parents had an added incentive to visit me and see their new grandchildren. Their visit was short and tense that following Sunday afternoon. We were both hurting: I was hurting because I wanted them to love my children and dote over their cuteness and sweetness which they could not do. They were hurting because they felt sorrow and pain over two children they desperately feared would not be raised as Christians. For the next few weeks, I mourned over the fact that I had two new beautiful babies and yet very few people with whom to share the joy. However, I knew God had blessed me and NO ONE could take that joy away from me.

20

Two months passed and it was time for me to re-address the issue of the bladder tumor. I had hoped and prayed during the pregnancy that the tumor would not affect the babies, and thankfully, it did not. However, it was now time to have the tumor surgically removed. I visited the urologist to set up a time for surgery. When he first spotted the tumor during the first few weeks of pregnancy, he reported that it was small enough to be removed without anesthesia, he thought. Now, though, it had been several months, almost a year, and he was not sure what to expect. The agreement was made with me that he would take me to the Operating Room. If the tumor was still small, we would forego anesthesia and he would promptly remove the tumor. If, however, there was growth of the tumor, then he would need to put me to sleep for the surgery. That sounded reasonable.

I remember awaking early, the morning of the scheduled surgery, showering, and then kissing Bob "good-bye". He made arrangements to stay home with the kids while I drove myself to the hospital. I was hoping for a short procedure that would have me home by early afternoon. I arrived at the hospital, nervous but ready to get the procedure over with quickly, I had hoped. As I was wheeled into the Operating Room at Tinker Air Force Base, I remember lying on the bed, talking to the anesthesiologist about the procedure while waiting for the doctor. I reminded him that anesthesia might not be needed. However, as soon as Dr. Lawson arrived in the OR and inserted the scope, I could hear him quietly pointing out more tumors that would need to be resected. He then walked over to the bedside and spoke to me quietly, "Marcella, we see several areas here we're going to need to address. So, I'm going to have to put you to sleep." I nodded and closed my eyes. The next moment I was aware of, I was being awakened by the anesthesiologist. He said I did fine, except for asking him to scratch my nose during the procedure. Then, a few minutes thereafter, Dr. Lawson approached me.

"Marcella, I think we're going to have to get a bit more aggressive with your bladder."

"What do you mean?" I groggily asked.

"Well, as in removing it. You had several serious looking tumors in there. Also, I think we're going to have to keep you overnight because the surgery was much more involved that I originally thought. Your bladder was actually perforated during the surgery."

"Okay", I limply replied.

As soon as he turned away, I began to feel warm tears down my cheeks. "Remove your bladder", "Stay overnight", "perforated your bladder", the words rang in my ears.

Who was going to watch my kids? My husband had to work. I couldn't ask Linda to take off work again and drive all the way from Tulsa! I had no other close friends and I was pretty sure my parents were not interested in coming to stay. I didn't want to have my bladder taken out! And, I certainly didn't want to deal with this now! Soon, I was wheeled into a regular hospital room where I lay sobbing while a technician stood by my bedside. I was feeling intensely sorry for myself and the more I thought about it, the harder I sobbed. He compassionately asked, "Do you want to talk about it?"

"Not really. You really don't have the time for all I could tell you."

"I've got all the time in the world."

"That's nice. But I don't think so."

"Well, in case you change your mind, I'm here." And he was there . . . he continued to stand there by my bedside.

I finally just started blubbering about all that had happened. It probably didn't make much sense, but when I stopped, he kindly said, "You know, I've had all sorts of problems, too. But somehow, they have a way of working out, you'll see."

Just then, a nurse entered the room, "Would you like to see a minister?"

"What kind?" I weakly inquired.

"I'm not sure."

I thought to myself, "What could it hurt? I'll ask him a few questions and tell him part of my story. It'll be interesting to see what he says." I waited all day, but he never showed.

An hour or so later, Bob called to check on me. He had found a kind neighbor to babysit for a couple of hours so that he could visit me in the hospital. He also called my parents and offered to drive to their house if my mother would agree to come to help with the kids for a few days. My father agreed to meet him halfway on I-40 and bring my mother to help. That was a huge relief! Then, shortly thereafter, the urologist made the decision that because Bob was an ER doctor, there was nothing the hospital could do for me that he couldn't do for me at home, so he agreed to let me leave that same day.

I returned home a little sore and tired that afternoon, but to a house full of happy and excited kids because Grandma had come to stay! As awful as that surgery was, it was nice to have my mother with us for a few days. She seemed to bond with the children—all the children—and her help was invaluable. We avoided the religion issue, for the most part, and it was nice to enjoy a mother/daughter relationship where I could rely on her for her love and help and she could provide the nurturing that only a mother can. I wished, so badly, that our relationship could remain intact, as it seemed for those few days.

There were complications from the surgery that involved more trips to the Emergency Room and more surgery. I was feeling weak and a bit worried, but my mother was there to care for the children and to give me support.

At the end of the week, when my father arrived at my house to drive my mother home, I hugged my mother, with tears in my eyes, thanking her for her help. My father chuckled a bit, and then he commented, "Marcella, I'll be really glad when you and the boys get back in church. I don't think Bob will ever go back, but I'll be glad when the rest of you do." I didn't say much, just nodded.

21

The following weeks proved to be challenging ones, as I was back and forth to the hospital for more bladder surgery due to previous surgery complications. The day before one of my surgeries, my parents stopped by the house to see how I was doing. I was tense and a bit high-strung. We sat in the family room, rather quietly, with not too much conversation. My father then cleared his throat: "Marcella, I just really wish you would come back to church. I think it would make all the difference in the world for you."

I began to choke up, "Daddy, I want you to know that I would love nothing more than to come back to church! I am NOT trying to be rebellious or hard-hearted. I hate not having a very good relationship with you and Mother. I miss terribly not having friends. I don't like the fact that I feel that everyone in the family is talking behind my back about me."

"Well, do you ever read the Bible any more?" my father questioned.

I glanced at Mom whose face was covered with her hands as she began to sob.

"Yes." I replied.

"Well, what about Isaiah 53? Don't you realize that verse is talking about Jesus? Don't you see that as important prophecy?"

"Well, I know that's what the church taught, but the Jews have a different interpretation of that which seems to make more sense." I nervously replied.

"Well, what's their interpretation? Where's your Bible?" my father asked.

"She doesn't have one anymore," my mother quickly interjected.

I went upstairs to get the red Scofield Bible that belonged to Bob and brought it to the family room. I explained that "he" had been mistranslated from the Hebrew language. It was actually supposed to read "they" and "they" referred to the Jewish people and that in order to understand Isaiah 53, one had to read the entire chapter, not just a few verses.

"Well, I don't think that's correct," my father replied.

"Who do you think would be more qualified to interpret the Hebrew Scriptures: Jews themselves or Christians?"

"The Christians," my mother confidently answered.

The temperature of the room began to rise. "I am more than open to consider other interpretations, but it just seems that no one is really interested in talking about this. I have said before that if you would like Bob and me to talk with your pastor or any other knowledgeable teacher, we would be happy to do that."

"Marcella, that wouldn't be possible. Bob said he was the smartest man in the world. You can't reason with someone like that.'" My father replied.

"He never said that!'" I responded in frustration.

"Yes, he did. I heard him. Didn't he?" turning to my mother for confirmation. She nodded her head adamantly.

"I was there, too, when we had that discussion. That is NOT what he said, but that's how you INTERPRETED it!" When my father had asked Bob many weeks earlier why we would not come to church with him, Bob replied that we had "covered that ground before." He went on to say that he believed he had studied as much or more than many Christian pastors and would be willing to debate any one who was willing to discuss problematic issues. However, my father had clearly interpreted that to mean Bob, my husband, viewed himself as "the smartest man in the world."

"No, he didn't!" I screamed. The sense of frustration and pain seemed to swell as we talked. "I want you to know that I love you and want a relationship with you and it pains me greatly what has happened, but I can't change the way I believe! I need help!" I sobbed. "I'm tired of everyone saying how bad they feel for me, yet no one seems to want to do anything about it except talk behind my back," I angrily retorted.

The room grew quiet. "Well, we better be getting back before the traffic gets too heavy. Rush hour will be starting soon," my father replied. "We love you, Marcella." Then, they left.

22

The subject of religion with my parents was not discussed again for a very long time. I continued to maintain a relationship with them, but never mentioned specifics of religion.

In May 1998, my family made arrangements for a transfer to Colorado Springs, Colorado, where Bob would be assigned as an ER physician at the United States Air Force Academy.

One morning, a few short weeks before the move, the doorbell rang around 10 am. I had just put the twins down for a nap, showered and dressed. I went to the door and there stood a young woman who, with her husband, had just days earlier looked at buying our house. She was holding a plate of delicate-looking, flower-shaped cookies. "I know this is going to sound really crazy, but I brought you these cookies. God wanted me to tell you that He loves you. I couldn't go to sleep last night because I couldn't quit thinking about you. It's nothing that you really said or did when we were here before looking at your house. It's just that God impressed upon me last night that you desperately need to hear that He loves you. So here . . ."

I looked down at the plate of cookies and up at the clear blue skies framing the woman's face. Somehow, I was incredibly touched that God would send a human messenger to remind me of His love for me. I began to cry. "Come on in," I whispered. We sat in the living room and talked while the twins slept and her husband waited patiently in the car. I related some of my trials the past couple of years. She listened quietly, assured me that God loved me and that she would pray with me and for me. Then, she left. That afternoon, as I shared the episode with Bob, he quipped, "She was crazy." Not to me—she was an angel.

23

In some ways, Colorado Springs was a refreshing break from Oklahoma City. Most of our neighbors did not attend church on a regular basis, and therefore, did not judge us and dislike us, as many neighbors in Oklahoma City had. In my younger years, I never thought I would be glad to have neighbors who did not attend church, but in this situation, it was welcome. As a family, though, we continued to struggle with where our niche was in the religious community. There was no observant Jewish community in Colorado Springs, and at this point, church was, obviously, no longer an option. We were aware of a Jewish community in Denver, but did not know how to pursue a connection.

Our Bible studies consisted mainly of what we referred to as "Torah Time." Each Saturday morning, we would gather as a family in our living room and study the Parsha of the week. Bob encouraged our boys to read and study by rewarding them monetarily if they knew the answers he asked them afterwards. They seemed to enjoy the weekly challenge.

In addition, we tried to observe the Sabbath, at least in part, by having a festive meal on Friday evenings and reciting some of the traditional Jewish blessings.

Two years earlier, our Jewish friends, the Rossios, had given us a book, entitled, "Friday Night and Beyond", by Lori Palatnik. It was meant as a going-away gift when we left Ohio. However, when they presented us with the book, my first thought was, "Why are they giving us THIS? We haven't decided to convert! What am I going to do with this?" Not knowing exactly what to do with it, I stowed it away in a lower dresser drawer, thinking eventually I would either toss it or donate it. However, as I began to, at least, consider the possibility of learning more about Judaism, I retrieved the book to take a closer look at it. It was actually quite helpful. Not only did it explain the significance of Shabbos (the Sabbath), but it even had recipes and practical tips for how to make Shabbos more enjoyable for the whole family. I began to refer to the book more and more often and actually enjoyed it. It was one of the few Jewish books I owned that I could understand, so it became a very resourceful reference book for me for many years.

As the weeks passed in Colorado Springs, I began to feel a myriad of emotions. After just a few weeks in Colorado, my urologist diagnosed me with more bladder tumors and recommended chemotherapy. I began to feel down and depressed that I had no one to babysit for me during the doctor's appointments and surgeries. I would remind myself that if I was still in church, someone would provide child care and meals for me. Now, there was no one. I did have kind neighbors who were willing to step in and help out, but I always felt rather awkward, calling someone I hardly knew, asking them to babysit for me all day while I had another surgery.

I began to mourn the loss of the relationship with my parents. Although we still communicated, mostly by phone, and with some summer visits, the relationship was not the same. The visits were more strained, the topics were cautiously guarded, and we both knew that I was not the same person I used to be—at least in my spiritual beliefs.

In addition, our family led a busy lifestyle, not unlike many other families. There were baseball and soccer games, the practices, and young twins who required a lot of attention. There was homework and housework and day-to-day errands and fatigue. I wasn't sure where our lives were taking us. I began to have serious doubts and resentment over the fact that my husband had initiated this journey and although I was trying to ride along, I was beginning to wonder where this road would take us. The ride was not too enjoyable for me at the moment.

I would waffle between wanting to take an extra step towards Judaism, then step back and wish that things were somehow different. I would ask why we couldn't just be Noahides (righteous Gentiles). They serve the one true God of Israel, but are not obligated to keep the 613 commandments given specifically to Jews. Yet, we found the Noahide community to be a very limited and diverse one. The only formal, organized Noahide community is in Tennessee. Moving to Tennessee to find out if this was "right" for us did not seem like a very viable option at the time.

Then, I would mourn the loss of community and friends I had in the church. I missed things as simple as getting up on Sunday mornings, dressing up, and having a special place of worship to attend.

My feelings of doubt and resentment and anger came to a head one morning as I worked in the kitchen and Bob was in his office. It was one of those mornings when we were both exhausted and things were not running smoothly. The phone kept ringing and the doorbell was chiming and Bob was having difficulty locating an important piece of paper that he thought had been on his desk.

"Where could it be?" Bob frustratingly yelled.

"What?" I tiredly asked.

"That piece of paper. I just had it here and now it's gone! It couldn't have just disappeared."

"Why don't you try standing up?" I asked, trying to help.

Silence.

"Why don't you try standing up?" I reiterated.

"I'm NOT going to stand UP!" Bob snipped. "It was here a minute ago and now it's gone."

"Well, I just know that sometimes when I lose something and I'm sitting down that if I stand up, it falls off my lap and is easier to see," I annoyingly reminded my husband."

"Well, I'm not standing up for that damn piece of paper." Bob replied.

"Another four letter word," I thought. "How can he be so spiritual, using language like that? I don't even know if I can trust him." In reality, Bob used very few four letter words, but in anger, he often would spit them out in frustration. He was constantly in a work environment that used different language than what I was raised with and I found the words incredibly offensive. My internal pressure button began to rise, but I remained silent until I heard Bob pick up the phone just a few minutes later.

"Hello?" . . . is Rabbi Twersky there?" he asked in a rather calm, polite voice.

"Yes, this is Bob Schiermeyer. Do you know when he might be back?" he continued to speak in a very cordial tone.

"Yes, I understand. Well, if you could just tell him I called, I would appreciate it. Thank you," he replied as he ended the conversation pleasantly.

I reminded Bob how amazing it was that he could talk in such a hurtful tone to me, but transform himself so miraculously, in a minute, over the phone.

Before I knew it, the steam began to overflow in me as I yelled, "I hate you, I hate you, I hate you! If I had a choice, I would have NEVER married you. I hate you for what you've done to my family, to me, to our kids, to our lives! If it wasn't for our kids, I would leave you NOW!"

Bob stood there solemnly, staring back at me. "What have I done to your family?" he asked somberly.

"You destroyed the relationship with my parents! It will never be the same. Our kids don't know where they fit in any more, and frankly, I'm not so sure I know what I believe any more EITHER!" as I sobbed uncontrollably.

There was a tremendous pause of silence between the two of us. Bob gently put his arm around me and we talked. There were apologies and a hug and I realized I didn't really hate him—much.

I did hate, however, the fact that I didn't know where our lives were headed and things were not making sense to me. I wanted peace and assurance that I was doing the right thing. I wanted to wake up one morning and have all the puzzle pieces fit together, but for now, that was not happening.

24

Our lives continued to reflect a desire to grow spiritually, but not knowing exactly what direction to take. One evening, Rivka, a wonderful woman whom I had met earlier in Texas phoned me. She had been introduced to me via Rabbi Singer. Her husband had been a former Baptist minister in Texas. Since meeting with her five years earlier, her husband, two sons and daughter-in-law had all undergone a formal Orthodox conversion in Flatbush, New York.

"How's everything going?" she politely inquired.

"Fine", I weakly replied. "How's everything with you?" I asked.

"Things are good, very good. We're very happy here. I just wanted to know where you are in your journey."

Plagued by fatigue and frustration, I spilled out everything. "I don't know if I ever want to be Jewish. It just seems like so much work for nothing. I clean and cook to prepare for Shabbos and then no one seems to even notice. We don't know how to pray the Jewish prayers and I don't know Hebrew and I certainly don't understand it when Bob tries to recite some of the prayers in Hebrew. It takes him forever to recite a prayer before a meal and then no one even knows what he said! Aren't we supposed to understand what we're praying? And another thing . . . when I see pictures of Jewish men with black hats and curls, it makes me very uncomfortable. They look different from anyone I've ever seen. I'm not so sure I want to be associated with someone that different-looking. Everything is so foreign. We have no one to learn with, no one to teach us, I'm just not sure this is for us."

Rivka paused on the other end of the line, "Well, let's start with Shabbos. You don't always have to have everything perfect. Just do the best you can.

Make sure you put a clean white tablecloth on the table and buy some challah loaves instead of making it if you have to. Keep the meal simple and enjoy being with your family."

"Well, it's just really, really hard doing that. Every time I start to do something, one of the twins starts to fuss or cry. I knock myself out to clean and cook a wonderful meal and most of the family, including my husband, eats a little bit, says they're tired and then leaves the table to recline on the couch. I end up with a sense of no gratitude and a lot of resentment!"

Rivka, careful with her words, said very little. I could tell she was taken aback at my attitude and harsh words. We talked a little more . . .

"As far as the peyos and the black hats, that's more of a tradition in Judaism than a requirement. In our community, I see all sorts of Jews. Some wear baseball caps, some wear yarmulkes, and some wear the traditional Jewish hats. It helps to identify the type of Jew they are."

"Well, it still seems kinda weird to me and bothers me."

"Marcella, the Jewish life is very challenging, but I wouldn't go back to the way things were for anything in the world. It's work, but it's very fulfilling."

As we concluded our conversation, I sensed that Rivka was disappointed in my attitude, but I was being honest and I needed a friend to listen. I couldn't help but wonder what she thought of me now.

25

The kids had just been put to bed in the evening, and the house had quieted down somewhat. The phone rang and it was Rabbi Eisemann from Ner Israel in Baltimore, Maryland. Rabbi Eisemann was probably the only rabbi, at the time, who we felt comfortable talking with. Our connection with him stemmed from his published book "Iyov". My husband had obtained a copy of his book several years earlier, while living in Ohio. He was so inspired by the book that he penned a letter to Rabbi Eiseman, making comments, and a few questions, about his book. It was from that initial contact that Rabbi Eisemann established a relationship with us. Rabbi Eisemann, as well as his wife, were kind enough to correspond with us and in some ways "take us under their wing."

We had not talked much with Rabbi Eisemann since the move to Colorado Springs, but he phoned us that evening to see how things were progressing. As Bob explained, "we were at a standstill." We had tried making contact with Rabbi Twersky in Denver, at the advice of some, but to no avail. We did not know until later that Rabbi Twersky was actually out of the country most of the time. Bob told Rabbi Eisemann of our struggles, and Rabbi Eisemann offered to arrange a meeting for us with Rabbi Feldheim in Denver, Colorado. Rabbi Feldheim was the principal of the Yeshiva Toras Chaim in Denver, the yeshiva for high school-age boys.

One week later, we found ourselves driving up I-25 to Denver to meet with Rabbi Feldheim. As we drove through Denver, I remember asking, "How much further?" It seemed we had already driven hundreds of miles. Finally, we made the exit onto Colfax Avenue and on down to Stuart Street where we located the Yeshiva Toras Chaim school. As we drove into the parking lot, there was a middle-aged gentleman, standing there, smoking a cigarette. "Please God, do not let that be Rabbi Feldheim," I prayed. The gentleman ushered us into the building and said that we could wait in the cafeteria for Rabbi Feldheim to arrive. (I breathed a sigh of relief.) It turns out that the gentleman that escorted us into the school was a professor of English studies, not Hebrew. As we waited, a few of the yeshiva students approached us, "Would you like something to eat?" they politely asked. "It's not very good, but you can have some." They smiled. We smiled back and continued to wait.

Shortly thereafter, Rabbi Feldheim approached us, introduced himself, and escorted us into a smaller conference room where we could discuss our situation with him. Bob talked briefly, and then I remember pulling out my short list, scribbled on notebook paper, of questions that I wanted to ask. "What do you say when people wish you 'Merry Christmas?'"

"What kind of music is appropriate for us to listen to—we no longer have Christian music and I don't know Hebrew too well, but I really miss music."

"How can we learn in a non-Jewish environment?"

"How do we teach sensitive topics in the Parsha to our children?"

The questions seem so trivial now, but they were pressing questions to me at the time for which I wanted answers.

Rabbi Feldheim responded kindly and methodically to each question:

"We all struggle with what to say when wished 'Merry Christmas'"…

"We just finished discussing music in one of our yeshiva classes. . ."

"It's important to teach your children by example…"

"Teach sensitive topics to your children based on their age. Sensitive topics can be explained in general terms…"

Rabbi Feldheim also suggested the possibility of attending classes at Rabbi Meyer's shul (synagogue) on the southeast side of Denver. It was much closer to Colorado Springs and "he offers classes almost every night of the week," explained the rabbi.

The rabbi's genuine care and concern for us gave me a taste of the kindness I had so often read about. At our request, he opened up the Jewish bookstore for us, even though the store was normally closed on Sundays. We found wonderful books and music that could nourish both our minds and our soul.

As we thanked the rabbi and drove back to Colorado Springs that evening, light snowflakes began to fall on the windshield. Colorado had not received moisture in weeks—we were experiencing major drought problems. Bob commented, "That almost looks like snow."

"Yea, right," I laughed. As we drove further, the flakes became heavier and heavier. Our speed slowed to 35 mph, the regular hour trip turned into two hours, and by the time we reached our exit, the car could barely pull us up the hill in the snow. The kids were ecstatic! The flakes were falling fast and furiously, to their glee and amazement. A snow day from school was already apparent. It looked as though our visit to the rabbi had not only brought us an end to our physical drought, but to our spiritual one, as well.

26

The following week, Bob decided to drive up to Denver, just to locate the Jewish community Rabbi Feldheim had mentioned to us. He met Rabbi Meyer, the shul's rabbi and received some brief information about classes. When he arrived home that afternoon, he walked into the kitchen with the information:

"I found the shul. It's actually pretty interesting. It's in a nice part of town and only about a 45 minute drive for us. Rabbi Meyer has a weekly Torah class on Wednesdays and I think I would like to try to go to it."

"That's nice," I added. I still was not sold on the idea of being Jewish. I had grown up in church, not a synagogue. The whole idea still seemed quite foreign, but if Bob wanted to go, perhaps he would gain something from the experience.

After a few weeks of attending Rabbi Meyer's classes, it was as though Bob had begun to have his insatiable thirst for Torah (the "Old Testament" scriptures as we knew them), whetted. He continued to go every Wednesday. It was literally the highlight of his week. He wanted to attend Sabbath services, as well. He spoke with Rabbi Meyer and Rabbi Meyer told him that he usually didn't encourage potential converts to attend. However, since Rabbi Eisemann had endorsed us, he was willing to let us be there. (Thank you, Rabbi Eisemann!)

Just weeks before I attended an actual Sabbath service, the shul sponsored a two-hour evening class on "Love, Dating and Relationships," presented by an out-of-town rabbi. I thought attending this class might be an easy to way see the shul for the first time and meet a few people. Again, I was still uneasy about attending a synagogue and being around Jewish people, not Christians.

I found myself pre-judging anyone who was not raised a Christian. I had been taught my whole life that Jews were not very nice people, that they had killed Jesus, and they really didn't know a whole lot about morals. As much as I tried to overcome that prejudice, it was very difficult, at first. However, the older boys agreed to babysit the twins in the play room at shul so that Bob and I could attend the class.

As we walked into the classroom, the first woman I saw was collecting money for the class. She was wearing a snood, a solid black nylon head covering, similar to a hairnet. I thought to myself, "Well, you wanted a head covering—but is this how you want to look?" The woman herself looked very pretty, but the snood made me think twice about covering my head.

I looked around the room. Many of the women were wearing slacks and jeans. I thought, "I thought Jewish women were supposed to be very modest. Why are they dressed this way?" Also, there were several men there, not wearing yarmulkes. Why not? I wondered.

Some couples looked religious, others did not. I couldn't figure out why everyone looked so different. It was later explained to me that Rabbi Meyer's shul was a kiruv shul—an outreach shul—in which people who were Jewish, but didn't know much about their heritage or practices, could still attend and learn about Judaism without feeling intimidated or unaccepted.

The class that evening was very informative. The rabbi shared some very practical tips for making relationships better and even threw in a little Jewish humor, as well. Even though it felt a bit foreign to be at a synagogue, it still felt encouraging to be at a house of worship. Because the synagogue experience was not too overwhelming, I felt I could at least try to attend a Sabbath service.

One Saturday morning in November, we drove from Colorado Springs to Denver to attend a Sabbath morning service at Aish Ahavas Yisroel.
I kept thinking, "I can't believe we're going to a synagogue. At least, it's a place of worship, but still it's a synagogue, not a church. I don't know what to expect, but here goes!"

We pulled into the parking lot next to the synagogue and I proceeded to gather up two diaper bags, snacks for the kids, and my purse. Then, Bob informed me that because money is not handled on the Sabbath, that I should probably hide my purse in the car. All seven of us filed out of the car and walked across the parking lot to the synagogue. Bob took the three older boys and sat with them on the men's side of the shul. (There is a wall or curtain, called a mechitzah, separating the men from the women during religious services). I took the twins and slipped into the women's side. Within minutes, the twins were fighting over who could sit on my lap. The service was quiet and respectful. Only the davening of the men could be heard until Dakota, followed by Danielle, pierced the solemnity of the service with their shrill cries for my undivided attention.

"I wanna sit on Mommy's lap," whined Danielle.
"Noooooo, get OFF!" screamed Dakota.
I so desperately wanted to witness this first service, but knew the twins' commotion could not be tolerated for very long. I tried to quietly slip out of the service, although when holding two two-year-olds and carrying two diaper bags, it was difficult to be very discrete.

I walked downstairs to the nursery area. It was a small room with a few colorful toys and some books and I put the twins down on the floor to play. There was another woman there with her daughter. She smiled, "Hi, I'm Michelle."

I smiled back, "Hi, I'm Marcella. This is my first time here. My husband and I are former Christians. We left the church about four years ago and because we're considering conversion, we came here." (Why did I always have to say more than what was necessary?)

"I'm a convert, too," Michelle calmly replied. "How old are your kids? Where do you live?"

We began a conversation that put me at ease and I realized that even someone Jewish could be nice.

The following week, we were back in synagogue. The same scenario developed with the twins not wanting to sit quietly so I found myself back in the nursery. This time, an unusually attractive woman came walking into the hallway, outside the nursery, looking as though she was prepared to teach a class. She spoke nicely to some of the other women. This woman struck me as someone totally put together. Her skin and makeup were flawless, her nails were manicured, her hair was neatly combed in place, and her clothes and jewelry were neat and modest, but very stylish. I remember thinking, "I want to know who that woman is. She exudes a beauty on the inside as well as the outside—and she's Jewish!"

Later, during Kiddush, Dakota was standing in line in front of this woman. He was taking several minutes, trying to decide which piece of fruit to take from the platter. I felt a bit embarrassed, when she looked at me and reassuringly commented, "I have kids, too."

"Sure she does," I thought. "Anyone who looks that good and is that put together probably couldn't have more than two children at most, and they're probably older."

Weeks later, I learned that woman was Rebbetzen Chaya Meyer, Rabbi Meyer's wife, and at the time, she had eight children, the youngest of which was less than a year old. She now has ten children and still looks as beautiful as ever.

After several weeks of attending shul, Rabbi Meyer requested that Bob and I make an appointment with him to further discuss our situation with him. Although he was aware of some of our background, he wanted to discuss specifics with us.

We met with him during the week, explaining again, only this time in more detail, how we had left the church. I could never talk much about my experience without emotionally breaking down somewhere in the discussion. It was a very painful experience for me, especially feeling a deep sense of loss. I was deeply mourning the loss of the relationship with my parents, and on a smaller scale, the loss of many of my friends. I felt I had somehow lost my identity. I didn't know exactly who I was or who I even wanted to be! I knew I wanted a deep relationship with God, but how to achieve that relationship was not clear to me. I was also grappling with the illness of cancer and chemotherapy and trying to make sense of how my physical illness played into my apparent spiritual illness.

Rabbi Meyer seemed genuinely interested in us. We discussed the fact that in just a few short months, Bob would be retiring from the military and have the option to move to a Jewish community. We were primarily interested in either Denver or Baltimore (Rabbi Eisemann's shul). Yet, I wasn't fully decided that I wanted to move to ANY Jewish community. We discussed our children. We also discussed the schools in the Denver area and what they had to offer. We discussed what path we should take, but again, Rabbi Meyer left the ultimate decision up to us—it was our decision what to do—and an easy decision it was not.

27

Weeks passed, and although Bob still enjoyed attending shul classes and services on the Sabbath in Denver, I told him that I wanted to wait. It was difficult to attend services with the twins, and because I spent many hours just waiting in the nursery for services to end, I told Bob I would rather stay home. Part of me wanted to be more involved; part of me did not. I enjoyed having what we called "Torah Time" with the boys. Bob would lead it on Saturday mornings. Each of the boys would be required to read the Parsha earlier in the week, then on Saturday mornings, we would read it together, discuss it, and then questions would follow. For each question answered correctly, there once again was a monetary reward. The boys seemed to look forward to the challenge of learning and I looked forward to the learning, as well, but also to the enthusiasm of the boys and the time spent together as a family.

Bob gradually quit attending Sabbath services in Denver for a while so that he could remain at home with the family. However, we still wanted to maintain some connection with the shul and Rabbi Meyer. Bob would continue to attend classes on Wednesdays at noon to hear Rabbi Meyer's teaching on the weekly Parsha. Also, if there was a particular class given in the evening during the week, he would also attend.

One particular evening, there was a special talk being given, just for women, by Lori Palatnik, on the role of women in Judaism. I was usually unfamiliar with the names of the speakers at the shul, but this name I recognized! Lori Palatnik was the author of the book, "Friday Night and Beyond," the book given to us as a gift by the Rossios several years earlier. I liked her book and was interested in seeing and hearing her in person. Therefore, that particular evening, Bob drove me to Denver, offered to take all the kids to Family Fun Center, while I enjoyed an evening at the shul.

Lori Palatnik's lecture was like water to my parched soul! Her words spoke to me in such a unique way. She related the story of her great grandmother and how she was willing to give her own life for the preservation of Torah in her hometown. Lori spoke about her own life and what it was like becoming more observant. She spoke of the role of Jewish women throughout history and their importance in preserving Judaism. Her words seemed so practical, yet so inspirational to me. As I rode back to Colorado Springs that evening with my family, I couldn't stop talking to Bob about how meaningful that talk had been to me. "You know, if I could just spend some time talking with someone like Lori, I think it would really help me."

I think God must have been listening.

28

More weeks passed, Bob's retirement from the Air Force was growing nearer, and a decision needed to be made as to whether we remained in Colorado Springs or attempted a move elsewhere to a more active Jewish community where conversion to Judaism could be a more serious option.

One Shabbos afternoon, while still living in Colorado Springs but visiting the Denver shul, we were invited to Bob and Rhoda Pitler's house for lunch. Mr. Pitler was former president of the shul, and his wife Rhoda was known to be a master at the art of hospitality. While visiting at their lunch table, the topic of conversion arose. Bob and I talked somewhat about our journey. Then Bob commented, "Well, I'm pretty sure it's not a question of 'if', but 'when' for conversion."

Really?! I thought to myself. I was a bit taken aback that he would make such a public statement in front of other shul congregants. Later that week, I confronted Bob. "I'm really upset that you would tell Mr. and Mrs. Pitler that we're converting. Don't you think you should discuss that with me and the kids first?"

Bob said, "Well, I am pretty sure that I'm going to convert. It may be when I'm 80 years old, but I really want to consider it. If you're not ready, then that's okay, but SOMEDAY, I want to seriously consider it."

Knowing that Bob was willing to wait until he was 80 took SOME of the pressure off of me and I was back to trying to decide what to do: stay in Colorado Springs or make the move to Denver. I knew Bob desperately wanted to consider conversion, but for now, he was leaving the ball in my court.

After much thought and prayer and discussion, Bob and I decided to attempt the move to Denver. My reasoning was that if we chose to stay in Colorado Springs, we would forever be saying, "We're thinking about conversion," but that would be it. We would never have a taste of real Judaism, we would always be on the outskirts of learning, but never directly involved. Our lives would always be hanging in the balance between Judaism and non-Judaism and never know exactly where we fit. It was a difficult decision, but we were assured by the rabbis that if Judaism was not for us, then we could turn back to being Noahides. Considering conversion simply meant that we were willing to learn more about Judaism and then decide if being an observant Jew was the right decision for us. If not, then that was okay. It was not the same analogy as in Christianity where if we chose to not be Christians, then our fate would forever be sealed in an eternal hell. This was not an irreversible decision.

As I shared our decision with Michael, our then 12 year old, he grew uncomfortably quiet. "I just made good friends with Ryan and some of the other kids and we're moving again." My heart sank as I wanted the best for him and the rest of the family and knew another move was not going to be easy for him—or the rest of us.

I began to cry and rub his back, "I know you don't want to move and I sometimes don't want to either. But, if we stay here, we'll always be wondering what Judaism is really like. We'll never really fit in here as far as being in a church or a synagogue. We'll never really have any friends that believe like we do. We'll have the baseball games and the school events and our neighbors who probably already think we're a bit weird, but we'll never know what Judaism is. If it's not for us, then we can turn around and make another decision, but we've come this far, we've got to try it. And as far as your friends, it's not as though we're moving out of state like so many other moves, you'll be less than an hour away. They can visit; you can visit; you can still stay in contact."

Michael remained quiet, but his silence seemed more like a silence of contemplation rather than rebellion. God blessed me with wonderful children. While many kids probably would have rebelled or given up on their parents, my kids remained respectful. Another move was going to be painful, but my children were willing to trust God, and their parents, that everything would turn out all right, eventually.

29

In May, 2001, the moving truck arrived at our house for another move—the seventh move since my marriage to Bob in 1984. (Pretty unbelievable, considering I grew up on a farm for the first 22 years of my life and never moved from there.)

The first few days after the move were stressful—the time during which Bob and I said, "I hate moving and I'm never moving again—never!" Many items of our furniture had either been damaged or completely destroyed during the move. Our new built-in microwave oven didn't work, we were starving and had no quick way to heat food, the security system was malfunctioning and kept going off at odd hours of the night—scaring us half to death, our phone number was wrongly assigned so that no one could call us—including repairmen, along with a few other minor glitches. I kept wondering if these were "signs", although somewhat minor, that perhaps we should not have made the move. I kept hoping to see a "sign" that what we had done was the right thing. Housing was much more expensive in Denver than anywhere else we had lived. Had we made a mistake? Did we do the right thing? Would our kids be happy here? Only time would tell.

The first few weeks in Denver felt almost like being in a new school. There were many new faces, some familiar ones, but nonetheless, this was a new community and a new experience for everyone.

Bob had accepted a position as an ER doctor in Denver just weeks before we moved to Denver. Although he liked the job, it was different and there were many adjustments to be made from what he was accustomed to in the military: different procedures, different personalities, different hours—plus it was somewhat different in the civilian world from the military environment in which he had been working.

Robbie, Michael and Stephen were busy scouting the neighborhood for famous athletes. With the Denver Broncos, the Denver Nuggets, the Colorado Avalanche and the Colorado Rockies all in the same town, they were praying that their chances would be enhanced to perhaps spot one of the better known athletes and procure an autograph or two. Turns out, that never happened, but the prospect was still enticing.

The kids soon settled into a routine. Robbie, our oldest, began working for Serge Herscovici, an attorney whom we had met months earlier at the shul. He was a Ba'al teshuva and was empathetic to many of the situations we were encountering.

Michael began working for David Solomon, another attorney from the shul, who also happened to need a part-time assistant.

Stephen was busy playing baseball, part-time, with the same team he played with in Colorado Springs.

The twins were three years old now and seemed to enjoy the adventure of exploring new parks and the new green territory within the neighborhood.

Before we moved to Denver, we would drive by Coral Place, a new development, and I would jokingly point and remark, "Bob, why don't we buy one of those homes and then we could just walk to shul?" Turns out . . . that's exactly what we did!

After living in Denver for a week, we could actually walk to shul. Observant Jews only walk on the Sabbath in adherence to the Torah laws that forbid driving on the Sabbath. (Bob walked early.) I could not believe it—we were finally in Denver, only a few blocks away from the synagogue, and here I was late for the Shabbos morning service, driving up Belleview Avenue with the kids on Shabbos. "What a wonderful beginning on our way to observant Judaism," I mumbled.

30

The next few weeks improved somewhat. I was actually able to walk to shul with all my children. It soon became apparent that there was so much to learn. But at least, we were in a Jewish community and in the proper environment for learning. We also soon discovered that there were many other Jews whose knowledge of Judaism was limited and that we could actually learn together, without feeling embarrassed or intimidated by our lack of knowledge.

Approximately one month after being in Denver, Lori Palatnik was scheduled to once again speak at the shul for a Shabbaton. I happily anticipated her visit, hoping that I could once again draw inspiration from her. The Shabbos she came to visit, I was somewhat flattered when some of the women mistook me for Lori. They didn't know what she looked like, but said they thought, after seeing me dressed up in pink, that I must be the guest speaker. It was nice to think SOMEONE thought I looked Jewish—the guest speaker, no less!

Lori spoke that day on her life and her family and I was again extremely intrigued by her. She was a person who had not been raised in an observant Jewish home, but had since become observant. The manner in which she talked and the stories she told were ones to which I could actually relate. I wished so badly that day that I could spend more time with her.

That evening, Lori's husband, Rabbi Palatnik spoke. He, too, was very interesting and someone from whom I could learn. He was warm and funny, but also very wise. That evening, the shul was packed for Shalosh Seudos. Apparently, I was not the only one who had been touched by them. When Shabbos was over that evening, I happened to be standing by Lori during

Havdalah. I thanked her for joining us and she replied, "You're welcome. See you soon."

"See you soon", what did she mean by that? Was she returning for another Shabbaton in the near future? Or, maybe that was just a phrase, "see you soon." The next day, I learned that she really did mean "see you soon"! My friend, Jane, relayed the message to me that the Board of Directors had voted to hire the Palatniks as part of the staff at Aish Ahavas Yisroel. Learning that news was like the excitement you feel when you meet someone you really, really like and hope that it's the beginning of a meaningful friendship. Perhaps Denver was going to be okay, after all.

When the Palatniks moved to Denver, I scheduled myself for every class they offered, whether it was on Shabbos or during the week. It was as though I could not get enough of their teachings based on Torah. I felt that even if I never converted, their teachings were true and practical, based upon sound Biblical doctrine. The truths they taught seemed to resonate within my soul in a way I cannot fully describe. Some of the Torah teachings seemed to be truths I had always known, but needed to hear verbalized. I found myself wishing that my parents could hear the classes, as well. I knew my parents would never get over the stigma of Jewish classes, but I still longed for them to hear what I was hearing.

Some of Lori's first classes dealt with "lashon hara". She taught the heaviness of speaking gossip and how Jews are forbidden to speak harmful words. Rabbi Palatnik taught classes on the Parsha of the week and he would always manage to illustrate the teaching with practical illustrations, and sometimes, with a little humor. I began to see that Torah was a real way of life and not some outdated material that had been replaced by the "New Testament". I began to see passages in the Tanach ("Old Testament") in a way I had never seen them before. Stories began to take on new meaning. In the church, we simply had the text of the "Old Testament" from which to learn. We did not have the advantage of learning from the rabbis about the Jews' rich background and history.

For example, I remember learning about Joseph and his brothers in a way I had never been taught. I was always taught that Joseph was guiltless and that his evil brothers sold him into slavery. I had never heard the side of the story of how Joseph encouraged his brothers' jealousy and how the brothers actually thought they were doing a spiritual deed by selling Joseph into slavery. I was fascinated by all the extra details of whom the people of the Torah were, and why they did what they did, and how the Jewish people could learn from their actions.

I looked forward to attending shul as much as possible. I began to feel a spark of spiritual excitement about learning more and more. It was also refreshing to ask questions of the rabbis and not be chastised for questioning their beliefs and religion. The rabbis did not seem angry or threatened by questions. In fact, they welcomed them! They would actually commend me by saying, "That's a very good question! Let's explore the answer." (Somewhat different from the Christian world I had known.)

I remember asking, "Why do you pray in Hebrew if you don't know what you're saying?" and "Why do the prayers take so long?" (as opposed to the prayer service in the Sunday church service which was never more than ten minutes), and "Why don't some Jews take their religion more seriously?" and "Why can't you do simple things like tear on Shabbos?" and "How in the world can you ever prepare any kind of meal for Shabbos if you can't cook?" (It certainly couldn't be a very delectable one!) The questions went on and on and on. Yet, the people I asked them to would reply with patience and understanding—a very refreshing response indeed!

31

Several weeks passed in Denver, and while my enthusiasm was increasing, the enthusiasm of our sons seemed to be waning. One Shabbos afternoon, Bob came home from shul, hot and exhausted and discouraged. "Why did we ever even move here? We spent hundreds of thousands of dollars on a house, moved here, and now the boys aren't interested in being here. They only go to shul to please us. They sit there in the service, looking totally bored, don't participate, and then leave as soon as the service is over."

In his frustration, Bob confronted the boys. "Why don't you like shul? What's the problem?"

"We don't know Hebrew and we don't know what's going on in the service," Robbie, our oldest replied.

"We don't know anybody either." Michael answered.

"Well, that's where you go and learn," Bob replied

"That's easy for you to say," Robbie replied, "but it's just hard for us."

The tense conversation continued with little resolve. After the boys left the room, I suggested that Bob and I talk either with Rabbi Meyer or Rabbi Palatnik about the situation and request advice.

Bob made an appointment that same day with Rabbi Palatnik to meet that evening after Shabbos in his office.

Around 9:30 pm, Bob and I arrived at Rabbi Palatnik's office. He kindly invited us inside his office to have a seat.

"So, how can I help you two?"

Before Bob could say too much, I interjected, "We really want our boys to be happy here and we're not sure how to help them. They've been through so many changes and we want to do the right thing. Robbie, especially, since he's the oldest, has had to adjust to so many new schools (8 schools within 10 years) and new friends, and now, a new religion. We're not sure now what to do," I sobbed to catch my breath.

Rabbi Palatnik listened intently.

"Let me think about this," he offered. "I'm not sure exactly what to tell you at this exact moment, but let me talk with my wife Lori and see if she has any insight and then we will talk again."

Bob and I thanked Rabbi Palatnik and left, feeling assured that he would have some type of answer. We weren't sure what—but something.

The following Shabbos, as I walked downstairs after Lori's women's class, she stopped me at the bottom of the first set of stairs and drew me aside.

"My husband talked to me about your son Robbie. You really ought to send him to Israel on the Men's Mission this year."

"We talked about that, but he has school and it would just be too hard for him to take the time off—especially ten days."

"You just tell the school that your son is going on an educational trip and that he will make up the work. The school is supposed to work for you—not the other way around."

I hesitated, "Well, I don't know."

"Israel is a magical place, I'm tellin' you! You need to send him, especially if you think you want him to be Jewish."

I hesitated again, "Well" . . . tears began to warm and swell again.

"Of course, if you're not even sure you want to be Jewish, then that could be a problem." Lori answered.

My throat tightened as I choked back the tears. Lori took me by the arm. "Come on," she said, "let's talk."

We walked back up the stairs to the loft where she had taught class. By now, all the women had exited downstairs for Kiddish and it was just us.

"What's up," she asked?

"I don't know. I think I want to be Jewish, but there are just some things that seem so foreign to me, like just now, the men rocking back and forth when they pray during services, and the prayer services are hard to understand and they go for a long time. Shabbos seems so hard to keep. There are so many laws and rules that I don't understand. I'm just not sure I could ever get used to that! And, there just seems to be so much to do that I begin to feel so overwhelmed."

"Let me tell you a story," Lori began. "When I was in seminary in Israel, there was a girl who was not raised observant, but she began to learn, and within weeks, she seemed to be doing it all! She would daven regularly, she would keep Shabbos to the minutest detail, she would learn as much as she could, but guess what . . . within six months, she was completely burned out. You can't expect to learn all there is to learn in a short period of time."

"You got that right," I nodded. "On the one hand, I find Judaism appealing and interesting, but on the other hand, I can find it so intimidating!"

"Let me tell you about the ba'al teshuva vacuum. Ba'al teshuvas are Jewish people who were not raised observant. When they start learning more about their Judaism, it becomes very scary for them, too. It's as though there's a huge schism between their old lifestyle and the one they're considering crossing over. They want to do it, they know it's the right thing, but it's also very scary leaving their old lifestyle behind."

I sat quietly, contemplating what Lori had said. I could somehow relate to that.

"I also imagine this is a harder time for you around the holidays, isn't it?"

Again, I choked up with tears, nodding my head.

"Let me tell you a story that might help you," Lori began. "I had a teacher in seminary who one day was teaching about David HaMelech. I, too, was at the point where I didn't know which way to turn. I was feeling depressed, and pretty much out of it that day. I was just sitting in class one day, like this (arms folded), feeling exhausted and questioning what I was going to do. The teacher was saying something about David praising the greatness of the heavens and the stars, when he stopped and said, 'Lori, where are the stars?' I replied, 'in the sky!" (of course!)

"But, can you see them?" he asked.

"No, not now," I (Lori) said.

"Only when it's dark, can we see the stars, he said, "just as oftentimes in our life, only when we experience darkness, can we see light and clarity."

"I suddenly realized that story was for me," Lori spoke softly. I nodded to her, this time with tears of appreciation.

Our talk had lasted the entire duration of the Kiddush meal downstairs, so it was time to walk home for Shabbos lunch. I walked home by myself that day, thinking, "I finally was able to speak with Lori one-on-one and she actually cares about me—even though I'm not Jewish!"

As I began to prepare lunch, Robbie walked in the kitchen minutes later. While I had been talking with Lori, he had been talking with Rabbi Palatnik. Rabbi Palatnik had convinced Robbie to attend the next Men's Mission in February.

"What?" Bob asked in surprise. "You want to go now?"

Robbie nodded his head. The dilemma was that although Robbie had changed his mind about going to Israel, Bob was now locked into his work schedule for the ER and was unable to accompany him on the trip, as he so much wanted to do. Bob had seriously considered the trip with Robbie earlier, but when Robbie said he was not interested, Bob proceeded to commit to a February work schedule. Robbie could still go on the Men's Mission, but he would be the youngest participant and knew the older men of the shul only by acquaintance, at best.

After much deliberation, Robbie still signed up for the trip, arranging to meet Avraham Rossio, in Washington, DC, on the layover flight to Tel Aviv. Avraham was the 16 year old son of the Rossios, the same family who we knew in San Antonio as neighbors and who had since become observant Jews. Mr. Rossio was also the one who had provided us the "Let's Get Biblical Tape Series" by Rabbi Singer. Robbie and Avraham had played together as best friends in earlier years and now they were reuniting again for their first trip to Israel. Mr. Rossio, who also had never visited Israel, agreed to accompany the boys on the trip.

Robbie enjoyed the enrichment of the Aish classes, the sightseeing, davening at the Western Wall, and Shabbos with Chassidic rabbis, but he didn't return home, wanting to convert. Rabbi Meyer wisely counseled us that if Robbie showed resistance towards conversion or attending shul that, as parents, Bob and I should not force the issue. Conversion was a serious issue into which no one, who is not Jewish, should be coerced into doing. Therefore, the issue of conversion was not forced upon Robbie. Bob and I knew he had made a sincere effort to understand Judaism and to also respect us as parents, but conversion was not for him, at least not for the present time.

32

Even though my son Robbie chose not to convert, I will always be thankful for the experience he shared. Before Robbie left for Israel, Lori Palatnik shared with me that many people leave notes to God in the crevices of the Western Wall. They believe that there is a special power or attention given to those special prayers inserted into the Wall.

"If you have anything in particular that you've been praying for, you should write it down and give it to Robbie." Lori said.

There are many things I had been praying for, but one thing in particular I especially wanted: to be healed from the bladder cancer. From the time of the first diagnosis, I had gone through numerous checkups and approximately ten different surgeries to remove the tumors. I had received chemotherapy and I so much wanted to be healed, not just for me, but so that I could be a healthy wife and mother, as well. I continued to have a twinge of guilt over the fact that I had prayed to God to die, and those prayers had been prayed in the bathroom. Now, the fact that I was experiencing cancer and bladder cancer, no less, seemed a little more than coincidence. However, I placed the prayer I had written in a small white envelope and asked Robbie if he would take it with him to Israel. Just before he left Israel, he took the note and placed it in the Wall.

Robbie returned from Israel in February, 2002. I was scheduled for my urology/oncology appointment in March. When I went for my appointment, I was still nervous. I had actually gone two years without a recurrent tumor, thank God, but if one was found, I knew it meant the whole routine all over again: three month checkups, surgery, and chemotherapy. The options were not appealing. When Dr. Crawford of the University Hospital in Denver began the cystoscopy to survey my bladder, I prayed hard, as always. On the little TV screen mounted above my stomach, it was not uncommon for the urologist to point out to me, where previous resections had been made, and where there was considerable scar damage and often inflammation and redness. This time, when Dr. Crawford placed the probe into my bladder and flashed the image on the screen, he smiled and commented, "Your bladder looks great." He then paused and said, "You would never know you had anything done." As I lay there, grateful and relieved, I answered with a smile, "Thank God."

Note: It has now been over eleven years since a tumor recurrence. My urologist told me that once a patient reaches ten years, they are considered totally cured of the cancer. I thank God every day for life, for health, and yes, for answered prayer.

33

As we continued to live in Denver, things began to take on more of a routine. It felt good to attend shul each week. I especially looked forward to Lori's classes and the rabbi's shiur (talk) each week. In some ways, I actually felt "at home".

The rules of modesty within Judaism were especially comforting to me. I grew up in a home where I always wore dresses, never jeans or slacks (in my high school years, my parents relented and allowed me to wear dress slacks), but for the most part, modesty was the rule in our home. I was often made fun of at school, and even in the church, for my mode of dress. Yet, in the Jewish community, I fit right in! No one—at least in an observant shul—was going to fault me for wearing a dress! And finally, after the agony I experienced earlier in the church of covering my head, I could practice without reserve! Again, no one was going to make fun of me for wearing a hat, or a scarf, or even a wig! In fact, it was encouraged!

On many Shabbos evenings, we were invited to the Palatniks for dinner. It was such a contrast, spending an actual Friday evening with an observant Jewish family, as opposed to how my family did it all on our own before living in a community. Everyone seemed happy and relaxed at the Palatniks, instead of being uptight and tense, as it so often was at our own table, especially for me. They prayed, they sang, they told great Hashgoka Pratis (God's Divine Providence) stories, and ate delicious Shabbos treats. It was always such an enriching experience for me. I wanted to learn more.

I spoke with Lori about being able to learn one-on-one with her. She explained to me that learning partners, or chavrusas in Hebrew, have to be two people who "click". In some ways, it's like a marriage. Either there will be a bond in which the two people can share trust and understanding between each other or there will not be. Fortunately, for me, we "clicked". We set up a routine of learning together every Tuesday and Thursday, at my home, from 9:30 – 10:30 am. It seemed so ironic—here was Lori Palatnik, the woman who had written the book "Friday Night and Beyond." I had almost thrown the book away, years earlier, and now here I was learning with her one-on-one, face-to-face in my own kitchen!

We studied many things: the laws of Shabbos and Jewish holidays, the laws of family purity, kashrut, and other pertinent Jewish topics, but many times, our discussions centered around either the practicality of Judaism and how to do the things that are required of a Jewish woman, or the frustration and despair I often felt trying to understand and put into practice many of the things I didn't grow up with.

To begin with, we spent much time studying the laws of Shabbos. Many of the laws concerning Shabbos were difficult for me. When I was a Christian, I thought I was keeping "the Sabbath" by not shopping or doing ordinary activities on Sunday. I thought by going to church, enjoying a nice meal, and perhaps a Sunday afternoon nap was how one properly kept the Sabbath. Hearing all the Jewish laws, both written and oral, about how to keep the Sabbath properly became overwhelming to me. Rules such as "you don't tear toilet paper or aluminum foil on Shabbos", and "you shouldn't turn lights on or off on Shabbos, including refrigerator lights and freezers", and "you shouldn't apply fresh makeup on Shabbos," and for sure "you shouldn't cook anything!" I kept thinking to myself, "How in the world can ANYONE do that?"

One Friday afternoon, as I was busy cleaning and preparing for Shabbos, I began to feel the familiar stress and fatigue that was so common for me before Shabbos. As I vacuumed and picked up clutter and cooked for Shabbos, as well as watched the kids, there was Bob: seemingly oblivious to everything, with his feet propped on the couch. He had worked a long week in the Emergency Room with 12 hour shifts and was due a rest. However, I was quietly fuming inside. "How can he sit there like that, with his feet up, while I slave away in the house, trying to prepare for Shabbos—a practice he initiated first, not me—and not feel any obligation to help?" If looks could kill, he would've been dead by then.

Tears and emotion swelled again, and for the moment, all I could think of was how much I would like to pack my bags, leave the house, and not come back for a very, very long time. Perhaps I could spend the evening in a nice hotel room, all by myself—a very tempting thought.

The air was a bit tense, to say the least, between Bob and me for the rest of the afternoon. Shortly before Bob and the boys prepared to leave for shul

Friday evening, Stephen yelled to me from his downstairs bedroom, "Mom, I don't have any clean clothes to wear for Shabbos!"

"I don't either", echoed Michael.

That was it. I marched angrily downstairs and exploded. "Well, that's just too bad! Did you ever think about doing your own laundry? Hmm? And, did you ever think about helping me, BEFORE Shabbos, so that I might have time to help you? If you think Shabbos is just about having everything delivered to you on a silver platter, well, it's time to wake up! From now on, you can get everything yourself! I'm not your servant as you seem to think!" Amid, a few other shrill words and screams, I marched out of their room, feeling exhausted, angry, and worn. Shabbos was coming, whether I liked it or not, and this was one time, I was not prepared.

When Bob and the boys returned from shul that evening, the table had been set and prepared for Shabbos, and I told myself I was going to control myself—no more yelling, no more harsh words, and no more conflict that evening. Of course, as I sat at the table, the mood was somber, at best.

As we sat around the table, passing the food, no one spoke more than necessary. Finally, Robbie, in an effort to break the ice, spoke. "Mommy, have you had a chance to do any more reading in that book you just bought?"

The book was "Patience" by Rabbi Zelig Pliskin. "I read a little of it yesterday morning, but none since then," I answered. I took a quick glance at Bob, then the boys. Realizing they probably wished, more than anything, that I had read the book and learned from it, I began to see how humorous Robbie's comment had been. Bob was trying to stifle laughter, and then, the boys began to giggle.

"Okay, guys." I smiled, "Maybe I should go read." The tone of the evening lightened and we finished the meal on a solid note.

The issue of trying to prepare for Shabbos, while maintaining a clean and happy home was one of great difficulty for me. I felt as though I spent my whole week, every week, focused on nothing but cleaning and cooking.

This was an issue I discussed regularly with Lori during our morning learning sessions. "I know," Lori would comfortingly say. "The first year I was married, I would cry to my husband, 'My whole life is Shabbos!' " She told me it seemed there was no time for anything else other than cooking and planning for guests. Lori's suggestion was that I hire a housekeeper and relax more about the food and the meals.

"But, we don't have the money for a housekeeper! This house is so expensive and kosher food is so expensive and I would feel guilty for hiring a housekeeper."

"Well, then why don't you consider down-sizing to a different house?" Lori asked.

"I don't want to move. I like our house. Moving is so awful. I just can't go through it again right now."

Lori had more patience with me than imaginable. I had a dilemma for her every solution. Fortunately, she continued with practical solutions for my every dilemma. I learned lights could be put on timers, special make-up could be applied for Shabbos, pre-cut paper towels and toilet paper are available, and food can be cooked in a crock pot before Shabbos and left warm, or set on a blech.

In the area of housecleaning, Lori loaned me her housekeeper for Fridays. Once her housekeeper moved, Bob agreed to cleaning help every Friday. The cleaning crew transformed the house every week, just in time for Shabbos. The stress level in our household went down considerably, while the level of Shalom Bayis went up dramatically.

Another issue discussed with Lori was how to cook kosher food for my family. My kids, and husband, were already picky eaters.

I was already a bit uneasy about visiting other people's homes because of an earlier experience while living in Colorado Springs. A couple from the shul had invited us to join them for Shabbos lunch. The experience was quite enjoyable, but true to my children's nature, they ate very little. As I buttoned up their coats to prepare to leave, Stephen asked, "NOW can we go to Burger King, Mommy?"

Now that we were trying to eat only kosher, and many new cultural dishes were being introduced, meal time was challenging. It was incredibly frustrating to spend hours on a new recipe, only to have it completely untouched by my family. It was even more embarrassing to eat out at someone's home for Shabbos. No one liked gelfite fish, or any other fish for that matter, except for my husband, and no one liked onions, salads, or kugels, except for me. We were a complicated clan of seven to invite and I would not blame most people if they did not want to invite us back for a second time.

I shared the dilemma of food with Lori, whether at my home or someone else's. She reassured me her kids were picky eaters too. She suggested to keep the food simple for the kids and cook whatever I liked for myself. She began to invite my family often for Shabbos meals. Her matzo ball soup became everyone's favorite. She also made yummy challah and chicken and potatoes and desserts that everyone would eat! We began looking forward to going out instead of always staying home.

Somewhere, along the line, most of us even learned to like gelfite fish. I learned that there are more ways to serve gelfite fish other than the beige-looking fish out of the jar. The first time I purchased gelfite fish at the grocery store, the bagger picked up the jar, examined it carefully, held it about two feet above her head, then exclaimed "Ewwww, what's THIS?!" Being embarrassed, I replied, "jell filthy fish". Needless to say, not only could I not eat it, I couldn't pronounce it either.

I also began to learn that eating at someone's house for Shabbos was not just about what food we would eat. It was about being able to recognize the Sabbath for the special day it is. It was about praying and singing and hearing the special words of the Parsha for the week. It was about encouraging one another and feeling a sense of friendship and love that, otherwise, we could overlook during the other busy days of the week.

It was also about keeping God's commandment to "honor the Sabbath."

Learning how to keep Shabbos became much easier with Lori's guidance. But just as I was beginning to understand and appreciate Shabbos, then came the challenge of the Jewish holidays.

34

I soon learned there was a huge difference between celebrating Christian holidays and Jewish holidays.

Growing up in the church, we celebrated two big holidays: Christmas and Easter and there were no restrictions on our activities. We could drive, cook, talk on the phone--whatever we wanted. Of course, we would go to church, read a few scriptures, pray, but then go home for fun and celebration.

In Judaism, I learned there are numerous Jewish holidays, as well as complete fast days. Some of the holidays last, literally, for days. There are prayer services that last for hours, not minutes. There are restrictions involving driving and cooking and regular day-to-day activities.

My family attended our first Rosh Hashana (Jewish New Year) services at the Red Lion Hotel in Denver. Since the shul's facilities were not large enough to accommodate huge holiday crowds, services were scheduled at the hotel and rooms were reserved. Because Rosh Hashana is a yom tov, I learned many of the same restrictions as Shabbos applied to it. For example, there should be no driving, no turning on and off of lights, no cooking, etc. Since my family was new to the whole experience, we decided to try to make things as easy and pleasurable as possible for everyone. So, for the first evening, after the davening, we gave our boys money to order room service (chicken nuggets, fries, and Cokes), and asked them to babysit the sleeping twins while Bob and I attended our first traditional Rosh Hashana meal. I found all of the Jewish customs very different. Some were quite appealing while others were downright disgusting. Dipping apples in honey seemed an appealing tradition as was the dipping of round challah in honey. The eating of celery (for a raise in "celery" for the New Year) or the eating of pomegranates to symbolize the 613 commandments was quite engaging, but the placement of a big dead fish head on the table was hard to swallow—literally. A fish head, though not required, is often placed on the table at Rosh Hashana to symbolize the role of a Jew in leading (with the head), rather than following. The explanation of all the foods and why Jews ate them seemed to take a very long time, considering it was already late and I was tired, probably just as much emotionally as physically. Then, the main meal arrived. The food was cold and I was disappointed. The meat was tough and the vegetables were unappealing and I kept thinking how we had spent a lot of money on such a bad meal. I also asked myself, "What did I get myself into?" As it approached midnight, I asked Bob if we could just leave early and go back to the room to check on the kids and go to bed. He relented as he was tired too. We walked back to the room. I don't know what Bob was thinking, but all I could think of was, "I don't think I want to be Jewish."

The next morning, Bob arose early for davening. He first went downstairs, into the dining hall, to grab a bite to eat before several hours of prayer. However, he was stopped short by Serge Herscovici. "Bob, men usually don't eat anything before morning prayers."

"Oh, okay, I guess I can wait," Bob replied glumly and hungrily.

Several hours later, I dressed and went downstairs with the kids. The older boys went to class. The twins wanted to stay with me. I attempted going into services for prayer, but Danielle and Dakota wanted my attention. I tried going to classes instead, but again, they vied for my attention. The morning was spent, walking back and forth in the lobby, talking to a few moms, and watching Danielle and Dakota. It was one week after 9/11, security was high and I still felt very uneasy, especially being in a hotel for a Jewish holiday.

Lunchtime finally rolled around, but again, having a family that won't eat fish, salad, or kugel, there wasn't much else to choose from. I turned to Bob, "Can we leave now?"

Although Rosh Hashana is a two-day holiday and was far from over, I wanted to go home. None of us had slept well, the food left much to be desired, and somehow during the Jewish holidays, I sorely missed my own traditions. Since we weren't Jewish, we technically weren't breaking any rules and, to be honest, I was seriously questioning if I really wanted to be Jewish.

I knew the next test in Jewish living would soon come with the observance of Yom Kippur, just one week later. Again, services were scheduled at the Red Lion Hotel. My family made plans to attend, although I was going with a deep-seated sense of dread. This holiday, as far as restrictions, would be the same as Rosh Hashana, except that it was also a full day of fasting. When prayers were concluded that evening, there obviously was no meal. I fed the kids (as they were allowed to eat), and then tucked them into bed, hoping for a better experience with Yom Kippur than Rosh Hashana. However, as I tried to fall asleep, Danielle began to groan deeply in her sleep beside my bed. I rubbed her back, thinking she was having difficulty adjusting to a different bed than her own. However, by 2 am, when she continued to groan and whimper endlessly, I held her to my chest. She was burning with fever. "Now what do we do?" I asked as I nudged Bob awake. "Feel Danielle, she's burning up." We both sat up in bed. "Is there somewhere we can go to get Tylenol?" I asked. Bob and I looked at each other questioningly. It was 2 am. Did we want to wake someone up in the hotel to see if they had medicine? The answer was obvious. Bob dressed and drove to a 24 hour Wal Mart, just a block away from the hotel.

While I knew we were not Jewish, somehow I still felt a compromised sense of guilt. Because we were not Jewish, we technically were not breaking any rules. On the other hand, if I really wanted to practice being observantly Jewish, I felt I was not doing a very good job. Danielle responded well to the Tylenol, but unfortunately, was still contagious. So, for our first Yom Kippur, Bob and I took turns staying in the hotel room with Danielle while the others went to pray or attend class. By mid afternoon, I could not stand the hunger. I could not ever remember fasting before in my life. Because the kids were eating chips and peanuts and M&Ms, I finally broke and ate some crackers and candy and drank some water. Again, I felt guilty. I wasn't a Jew, but I sure wasn't doing a very good job of practicing as one, either. By late afternoon, I was ready to go home—again. Because Danielle was sick, Bob agreed, and again, we packed up and went home EARLY.

"Well, at least, that's over for another year," I thought, only to be reminded that Succos was right around the corner in another week. "Well, all we need to do for that is to eat in a succah!" I wrongly thought.

The first day of Succos, I could hear the clicking of Bob's dress shoes across the hardwood floor. Then, dressed in his suit, he stuck his head into the laundry room, "See you later!" he called.

"Where are you going?" I asked curiously.

"To the shul."

"To the shul? What for?" I asked.

"Succos is treated just like a Shabbos. They have the normal prayer service, as well as extra prayers."

"You're kidding," I responded incredulously. "Do they do it EVERY day of Succos?" (Succos is an 8-day holiday.)

"Yea, they do." Bob smiled.

I could not believe it! The holidays were much different than anything I had experienced growing up. At the end of the Jewish holidays, I felt deflated and exhausted. How could I ever learn all there is to learn about Judaism? There is so much! It seemed as if the holidays went on and on and on-- forever! How could I ever learn to practice all the restrictions? How could I learn to actually enjoy the holidays instead of dread them? They seemed so foreign to me, and to be honest, not so fun.

As Lori and I discussed the holidays, I complained, "Maybe I just don't have the stamina to do this! The days seemed so long for me. I felt like I should have been in the services praying, but oftentimes, I found myself doing nothing, other than feeling guilty."

Lori tried to encourage me by informing me that the requirements for a woman are much different in Judaism than for men. For example, on Rosh Hashana, the main requirement for a woman is that she hear the sound of the shofar (ram's horn). The explanation for hearing the call of the shofar is that it is a call to teshuva. Teshuva is a special word, often translated as "repentance", but literally means "return," and refers to "returning" to the path of Torah ethics and spirituality. By hearing the shofar, Jews are not only returning, but remembering their Creator. For Yom Kippur, a woman needs to fast. On Succos, she needs to hear a blessing recited in the succah. There are requirements for every holiday, including Purim and Passover and Chanukah, but the spiritual necessity of prayer and shul attendance is much less because of the inherent spiritual nature of a woman. I felt a little better, but I knew my journey towards spiritual clarity was far from over.

Ironically, during the holidays, I continually reflected back to the stern reprimand my mother gave me many years earlier, as a younger woman. She reprimanded me for "always wanting to have fun" without responsibility or maturity. Had I remained that way? Was fun my main motivation for everything?

35

The most challenging of all holidays was Passover. This was the "big one." Passover made me keenly aware that I was not Jewish. I was overwhelmed by the cleaning and the food and the seder. Passover cleaning involved a thorough inspection of the entire house, including the garage, for chametz. (Chametz is forbidden on Passover and includes any leavened product.) Weeks before Passover, Jewish women are busy cleaning refrigerators, freezers, clothes closets, linens, beds, couches, and even their cars. All regular dishes used throughout the year must be stored away and replaced with clean and different Passover dishes. Not even a speck of chametz is allowed in one's home on Passover! Only "kosher for Passover" food is allowed. All other food must be eaten beforehand or sold. The special Passover meal eaten on the first two nights of Passover, called a seder, requires preparation of special symbolic foods, such as horse radish, romaine lettuce, matzah, charosis (a mixture of apples and wine), and hard-boiled eggs. In addition, most people serve a festive meal to celebrate the exodus from Egypt. After the two night seders, or meals, there are six more days of special Passover meals. After learning about the preparations, I literally did not know where to start.

The first year in Denver, Lori advised me to keep things simple: "Just put away, or use up all of your bread and cereal and other flour products from your pantry. And, try to eat only non-bread products during the holiday."

That sounded simple enough. Just put away the bread and eat non-bread products! How hard could that be? But, in all the frenzy of observing the other women in the community preparing for Passover, I became paralyzed.

Each day before Passover, I would think, "Okay, today is the day. I'll get everything organized and put things away." But, somehow, distractions stole the time away. Whether it was from helping other friends clean, or watch their children, I'm not sure. All I know was that Passover was upon me and I had done nothing. The bread, the potato chips, the cereal, all still remained, staring at me on the pantry shelves.

Feeling guilty, I reasoned that even though the bread products remained in the pantry, I could still serve my family non-bread products. However, after about three days, I was out of options of what to serve. We were already tired of potatoes and matzah pizza. What else could we eat? It was so bad that on Shabbos morning, I found myself taking out a pan and cooking lasagna for lunch. My daughter walked into the kitchen, gasping, "You're not supposed to be cooking on Shabbos!"

"I know," I replied, but I don't know what else to do! "Remember, we're not Jewish yet. It's okay." However, deep inside, I felt an overwhelming sense of guilt.

The cleaning and cooking were overwhelming, but the seders themselves were intimidating for me, too. I had trouble drinking four cups of wine. Because I grew up not drinking any alcoholic beverages, it was hard to overcome the stigma of drinking alcohol. Plus I didn't like the taste. I tried just drinking grape juice, but even that was difficult when required to drink four cups. I later learned that one only has to drink approximately four ounces from each cup. However, our hosts tended to use very large glasses and each "cup" seemed to be equivalent to several ounces.

The seder plate contained several foods representative of the Jews' exile in Egypt. For example, there was a mixture of apples, nuts and wine, called charosis, that symbolized the mortar the Jews used in Egypt to build bricks. There was a small bowl of saltwater to represent the tears of the Jews in Egypt. There was a shank bone to represent the lamb sacrificed on the eve of Passover. Among other items were large leaves of bitter lettuce and horseradish to represent the bitterness of the Jews' slavery. While I didn't care for their taste, I was told, "You need to eat 'this much' lettuce and horseradish." I kept thinking, "not if I'm not Jewish, I don't!" Then, there was the story of the Exodus that was read for two nights in a row. While the story is very beautiful and must be told, I kept wondering "how much longer?" and I found myself secretly peeking ahead to see how many more pages were left to be read. (It was always a bit more than I thought I could endure.) Perhaps if I had taken a nap, I would have fared much better. However, the situation was that I had tired children and I was a tired mommy —from Passover cooking and cleaning--and to be honest, I could not wait to finish. The seders usually ended around one in the morning, sometimes later.

I had the haunting feeling of "I will be so glad when Passover is over!" However, I would hear other friends comment, "I just loved our seder yesterday evening." Or one potential convert commented, "The seder is so natural for me. I feel as if I've been Jewish my whole life!" Obviously, I had not.

In my mind, I could hear my parents scolding me, "Marcella, it's never been right to drink. You know better than that. Those Jews have brainwashed you, for sure, now. You need to get out of that while you can."

"Being Jewish is so hard!" I would complain to Lori, afterwards.

"It's not hard. It's challenging," she would reply.

"Well, yeah, like I said, it's hard!" I responded.

"No, there's a difference. Rebbetzen Twerski teaches that you should never say Judaism is hard. That implies it is bad. Instead, you should say it is challenging."

"Well, you may use the word challenging, but it's just a matter of semantics. You can say challenging, but in the whole scheme of things, it's hard."

We bantered back and forth. Lori would never admit to Judaism being hard. Her position was that "hard" implies a situation that is not good and not worthwhile.

Later that day, I stopped by her house to drop something off. "Lori, I asked, how were your childbirth experiences?" Knowing she had had four C-sections, I baited her for her response.

"They were hard . . . challenging, very challenging," she replied.

Lori and I continued to learn between yom tovs. Even though I did not understand everything, I began to have an appreciation for what God had commanded the Jewish people to do. It was not always fun, easy, or convenient, but it was incredibly meaningful.

36

Even though I had left Christianity, I was still harboring the fear of hell. I had a deep-seated fear that if I were to convert to Judaism, and then fail to keep all the required commandments, then the consequences would continue to be extremely dire—that I could be cut off from the world to come forever. Rabbi Meyer explained that was not the case. If I purposely, and defiantly, chose to do something against the Torah commandments, then that could be a serious offense. But, failing to perform all the commandments perfectly, and without any mistakes, was human.

Lori reminded me continuously that God loved me and all that God requires is that I do my best in any endeavor. I might not understand every commandment. I might find some commandments more challenging than others, but all I have to do is accept them and then make my effort to perform them the best I can. God would take care of the rest.

I also came to the realization that Judaism is about God being involved in every aspect of one's life. If someone truly desires a deep relationship with God, then they have to be willing to accept "the rules". For every worthwhile thing in life, there is pain before pleasure. Whether it be children, or a successful career, or a relationship with the Almighty, there is pain before pleasure. I realized I could not expect a relationship with the Almighty to focus on me; it had to focus on Him.

I continued to vacillate between wanting to convert and not wanting to convert. "What about my sons? How would conversion affect them? What about my parents? How would they react to my acceptance of Judaism? What would they say if they knew we could no longer eat their food?" (My mother is an excellent cook and takes great pleasure in preparing special delicacies, so not eating her food could be painfully insulting.) Could I actually learn to keep the Jewish holidays the way they are meant to be observed? Could I actually refrain from eating bread and grain products, totally, on Passover? Could I actually observe each of the dietary fasts and not be tempted to cheat? Could I go forever without eating non-kosher food and give up such favorites as Pizza Hut and Kentucky Fried Chicken and resign myself to not being able to have an up-scale dining experience, at least for my anniversary? Would I be willing to send our kids to Jewish day schools and spend thousands of dollars for tuition and fund raising?"

After the Palatnik family joined the staff at Aish Ahavas Yisroel, approximately one year later, Rabbi Wasosky and his wife, Shana, were also hired to develop a youth program within the shul. While shul attendance continued to grow, so did the youth population. Rabbi Wasosky and Shana immediately began organizing programs for all ages. Their programs were interesting and much-needed. Because of their expertise in working with youth, Bob and I hired Rabbi Wasosky to work with our two sons, Stephen (6th grade) and Michael (8th grade). While Robbie decided not to pursue conversion, Stephen and Michael were still interested and Rabbi Wasosky seemed just the man to teach them. He began by teaching them Hebrew, then discussing relevant topics concerning Judaism. He often became a "sounding board" for the questions and concerns they had. After approximately a year and a half, Michael came to the conclusion that he wanted to follow the path of his older brother Robbie. He was happy with his position in life and did not want to pursue conversion. Again, upon the advice of the rabbis, Bob and I did not push him to continue learning with Rabbi Wasosky.

I struggled with Robbie and Michael's decision because I wanted the best for them, as any mother would. Part of my reluctance to pursue a conversion dealt with the fact that I wanted our family to remain intact. I didn't want my sons feeling as though they no longer belonged. Also, because of my upbringing in the church, it was hard to accept my sons not being involved in church or synagogue. I sought counsel from rabbis who basically advised me that, more important than my sons' involvement in a church or synagogue, was the example that Bob and I set for them. We can only impart the values and morals that we ourselves live up to in our own lives. It was impressed upon me that teaching values such as honesty and kindness and a love for God far surpass any membership in a church or synagogue. I was also reminded that my sons still have a part in the World to Come. Their lives may take different paths, but as long as they remain with a faith in God and seek to live good lives, they still will be rewarded.

Our third son, Stephen, continued to learn with Rabbi Wasosky for a few months. When Rabbi Wasosky's schedule became busier, Stephen began learning an hour and a half a day with David Ben Ami. David was an Israeli and a member of our shul. He taught Stephen a strong use of the Hebrew language and made learning more enjoyable than he could have ever imagined. They read Hebrew together, took field trips together--only allowing Hebrew to be spoken, and learned on a regular basis. The experience for Stephen was invaluable.

I continued to mourn the loss of the relationship with my parents. I remember one day in particular when I could not stop crying. Lori arrived for our usual learning session. Trying as hard as I could, I could not stop crying. The Palatniks had celebrated the bar mitzvah of their son, Zev, just two days earlier. Both sets of grandparents attended, as well as many other relatives and friends. Zev articulated his speech beautifully, and his grandfather related very poignant stories of his relationship with Zev. He told of how they went swimming and fishing together and how they had a special favorite chicken restaurant they would frequent together. It was nothing short of beautiful and tended to remind me of the relationship my father once shared with my children.

"Zev's bar mitzvah was beautiful. Even if we do convert and my children have a bar or bat mitzvah, I will never have what you have: the support and love of family—that special joy of having your whole family together to celebrate. It was so beautiful! For us, there will be no one." I continued to cry and sob and feel incredibly sorry for myself.

Lori quietly listened, "I don't know what to say. I really don't know what to say." There was nothing to say. I just needed someone to listen and she was there.

Many questions mulled over and over in my mind. While I was uncertain whether Judaism was really for me, I saw many positive aspects, as well. I watched observant Jewish people and somehow sensed that, although their lifestyle was a rigorous one, they seemed genuinely happy. They seemed to derive great joy from keeping the Sabbath and the Jewish holidays. Their lifestyles involved a tremendous amount of commitment and hard work, oftentimes amidst other obstacles. I witnessed men davening for hours, but they actually seemed to enjoy it and derive great meaning from the prayers. I would watch the women in the community invite several guests for Shabbos, sometimes every week. They might have had a difficult work week or sick children or other obstacles, but they still seemed to derive joy from the mitzvah of hospitality.

These Jewish people were truly genuine. I would have thought with all the "Jewish" requirements, the women would have looked bedraggled and run down and grumpy and that the men would look tired and depressed. Instead, it was just the opposite! The observant Jewish women were some of the most attractive women I had ever seen! They always appeared well kept, modestly dressed, and wore beautiful smiles. They worked hard at not speaking lashon hara and they even had a good sense of humor. The men actually appeared to be rejuvenated by their davening! I wasn't ready to make a commitment yet, but there was a spark that I could not deny.

37

Because the rabbis taught me that I didn't have to convert at any specific time, and although they probably wondered what was taking me so long, I chose to continue to learn and pray and attend shul services, but without any specific conversion commitment.

About one and a half years after living in Denver, there was a leak in my kitchen. Water from the upstairs bathroom shower had leaked through the ceiling and caused a need for major repair. A repairman came to fix the leak, but in the process, totally blocked off any access to my kitchen. I seized this as an opportunity to eat non-kosher food! Obviously, after living in the Jewish community for over a year, I had tried to eat only kosher food, along with my family, but I reasoned to myself, "I'm not Jewish yet. I'm not breaking any laws here. There's no way I can cook in my kitchen, so why not take advantage of the situation? There's a wonderful Chinese carry-out, located at King Soopers, right across the street. We can have convenience, as well as taste! I fantasized about Chinese food all day, what I would order and how much! When I parked my car in the King Soopers parking lot, I could smell sweet and sour chicken wafting from the little restaurant. I walked inside, already prepared to explain my dilemma should I be approached by anyone from the shul, but I was not. I walked up to the counter and placed my order for sweet and sour chicken, rice, beef, broccoli, and whatever else came with the biggest family special they offered. When I arrived home, I dove into the food my mouth had been craving all day. Wow—what a meal—I thought— until the next morning. I awoke, feeling a little nauseous, but thinking I was probably just confusing nauseous for tiredness and got dressed and left for the commissary (the military grocery store.) As I walked down the aisles, I became increasingly sicker and sicker. I had tons of gas weighing on my stomach and intermittent waves of intense nausea. I checked out with my almost empty cart and prayed I could make it home safely. I spent the next

24-48 hours, lying on the bathroom floor, dragging myself to the toilet every 15 minutes. It was the sickest I could ever remember being. My husband gently reminded me that perhaps HaShem was trying to tell me something. By the way, no one else in the family suffered a hint of sickness other than me.

After two days of intense sickness, it was Friday and the Palatniks had invited my family for Shabbos dinner. I was debating whether or not to go. I wasn't sure if I was contagious and didn't want to spread that horrible sickness to anyone else.

Friday afternoon, the phone rang. "Hello, Marcella?" Lori asked at the other end.

"Yes," I weakly answered.

"Are you and your family still coming for Shabbos tonight?"

"Well, I don't know for sure." I explained.

"Why, what's going on?" Lori asked.

I went on to explain to Lori the whole scenario of the kitchen and the Chinese food and the horrible sickness.

"What??? You ate treif food? You didn't just eat vegetables—you ate real treif? You ate meat?? I can't believe you did that! I can't tell you how many people have done that and become sick! You should've known better! I can't believe you did that! I can't believe you did that!" (I wished she would have refrained from saying that.)

I tried lamely to justify my actions to Lori, but to no avail. She was NOT very understanding. I gave up talking and just listened to her. I was sick and weak and mad at her for being so accusatory.

"Why are you so demanding of me, but you won't talk like that to people who are actually Jewish?" I asked.

She told me those situations were different. If I had any steam left in me, it would have definitely been smoking.

Minutes after our conversation, Lori sent chicken soup over to me, with a note saying "I'm sorry." I forgave her, eventually.

38

The Jewish way of life was an all-consuming thought for me. Between Shabbos and the Jewish holidays, as well as proper prayers in the morning, afternoon, and evening, not to mention blessings for food, blessings after going to the bathroom, blessings for nature, family purity laws, and laws of proper speech, I sometimes felt there was so much to learn that I would never be able to be a Jew.

"So, how long does it take before a convert can do everything?" I asked Lori.

"You will never be able to do everything," she answered. When my husband learned with Rabbi Noach Weinberg, he asked him the same question. The Rabbi answered him, "Not even I am doing all that is required."

"The Jewish way of life is a process. It's not all or nothing. You keep learning and doing your best. God loves you and will help you do what you're supposed to be doing." Lori advised me.

While Judaism seemed to have so much to offer and to learn, I would find myself feeling overwhelmed and discouraged. Did I really want to be Jewish? Did I really want to be obligated to do all the things that a Jew is obligated to do? The other roadblock I encountered was my previous experience in the church. I heard more than once, "The Jews just try to keep the Law. They are so caught up in do's and don'ts that they don't have a relationship with God." While I now knew that not to be true, the stigma of acts versus faith kept creeping into my mind.

Then, I would reflect on my thoughts as a young girl. Many times, at night, I would lie awake in bed, thinking about God, and wondering how I could best have a relationship with Him. Part of my thoughts stemmed from fear of what would happen if I did not serve God properly. I definitely did not want to end up in hell and burn forever and ever in a fiery furnace.

However, another part of me desired to do my best out of love for God. I knew God was real and that He loved me. I knew that He was my creator and that if anyone knew what was best for me, it was God. Before ever being Jewish, I remember wanting to connect through prayer and while I prayed spontaneously from my heart—the only way I knew to pray--I found myself reading Tehillim (Psalms) because I felt such a stronger connection through scripture. Somehow, it felt as though my prayers were taken to a higher level by reading prayers written by King David. I knew I was commanded to "praise the Lord with all my heart", but the Psalms seemed to reflect what I felt in my heart, but didn't know how to say. I was delighted when I learned that many of the Jewish prayers are taken from Tehillim! I remember wondering which shoe God would want me to put on first in the morning. I was told in Christianity that it didn't matter, yet in Judaism, I learned there actually is a right way to put on shoes! I even remember, as a 10 year old, being fascinated by a booklet the girls were given by the school health nurse. It talked about the importance of proper hygiene and how girls should care for their bodies as they grew into young women. I read the book many times as the concept of complete cleanliness for a woman was appealing to me. Then, as I learned the laws of family purity, I again felt a connection between my personal desires and the teachings of Judaism. Many times, in Christianity, I would hear sermons where the pastor would exonerate the congregation to live for God and to "be a lighthouse." Yet, I wasn't exactly sure how to do that. I knew I was supposed to read my Bible and pray and be nice to people, but where was I supposed to go from there?

Yet, here I was, now learning what God expected of the Jewish people. It wasn't just an outline. It was specifics: how to pray, how to keep the Sabbath properly, how to observe the Jewish holidays, what food to eat, what food not to eat, what words to say and not say to other people. Everything was there for the Jewish people! God loved His people so much that He gave them specific details on how to keep His law—His forever Law—and how to be happy.

While I felt inadequate in my learning process, I found God's laws to be what I had been looking for my entire life. God's Law told me exactly how I should live!

39

In April, 2003, just hours before the start of another Passover, the phone rang and it was Dr. Hoffenberg, urgently asking to speak with my husband. Apparently, there was a recent patient complaint filed against my husband concerning his treatment of a 15 year old drug addict in the ER. While I am not at liberty to discuss specific details, it was a complaint filed by the patient's grandmother, who happened to be drunk during the episode, and spewed many anti-Semitic comments behind my husband's back. (She knew he was Jewish because of his yarmulke.) Dr. Hoffenberg informed my husband that he was being placed on investigative leave until further details could be gathered. If timing is everything, then this incident could not have been better orchestrated. On the last day of Passover, my husband was called into Dr. Hoffenberg's office and told he was being permanently released as an employee of CarePoint (a company that provided ER doctors to some local ERs). There was humility, of course, along with anger and frustration at the situation, but what had happened, had happened—for a reason. We just weren't sure what the reason was. Now, it was time to deal with the implications and look for work elsewhere.

Several weeks later, at the conclusion of Lori's class on Shabbos, Lori announced the upcoming women's mission to Israel. The woman sitting next to me, EliSheva, leaned over and asked excitedly, "Are you going??"

I shook my head "no". She then exclaimed, "WHY NOT??!!"

Still feeling a bit worn, I retorted, "Because my husband lost his job and we don't have the money—that's why!"

"Oh, I'm so sorry, Marcella. I'm so sorry," she replied in shock and sympathy.

Not being able to control my emotions, I started to cry (again). Although I must have been known as the most emotional woman in the shul, people seemed to be understanding and nonjudgmental.

The class was over and as women filed out of the room, one of my good friends, Sandra, walked over to me. She hugged me and suggested, "Let's go for a walk." We talked and I shared with her the recent trauma of Bob losing his job.

I continued to share with Sandra the emotional roller coaster I had been on, trying to decide what the right thing in life is. I told her that in my mind, I could hear my parents saying, "You know the reason Bob lost his job is because you should never have been trying to be Jewish in the first place." I explained that no matter how old I am, I still want my parents' approval and it pains me greatly to know that I probably will never have it. I also wanted Bob to have a job, but didn't know if we would be staying or leaving Denver. The health group where Bob previously worked staffed the majority of hospital ERs in the Denver area.

Sandra was a very good listener. It helped to have friends like her. She asked me "How would your life be different if you were to convert now instead of staying the way you are?" Even though I had been concerned about my family, she raised a very valid point. Would things be that different if I converted? It was not as though my parents could be any less happy with me than they already were. And, it was not as though my sons would change much in their relationship either. We accepted them for their position and they respected Bob and me for ours. Somehow, I knew God had sent Sandra to me, at the right time, at the right place.

40

The next few weeks were spent job searching. There was an excellent opportunity for Bob, back in Ohio, not far from where we had once lived. The salary was literally twice the amount and the housing opportunities were much better there, as well. Bob and I would gaze over the internet at the available housing and daydream over some of those wonderful places.

Finally, a decision had to be made. "So, what do you want to do?" Bob asked me. "Do you want to move one more time?"

The thought was tempting . . . double salary, beautiful houses, a pleasant location, and "surely we would make friends, wouldn't we?" I reasoned.

Also, a decision finally had to be made as to just how important Judaism was to us. Did we really want to continue the pursuit of conversion, or perhaps concede that conversion just wasn't for us? We could go back to eating all the non-kosher food we once enjoyed, not to mention the unlimited restaurants and cuisines. Our kids could play more sports, even on Saturdays and not feel guilty, we could buy a beautiful house at a much lower price, and life could be much easier for us in many ways. What was to be?

On the other hand, where would we ever find a shul like Aish Ahavas Yisroel? The Meyers, the Palatniks, the Wasoskys—what shul would ever have a staff like that? And the friends we had made were genuinely precious. Did we really want to leave all that behind to start over, or perhaps, forsake entirely?

I was forced to confront myself with what was really important for me. Was eating non-kosher food and going to nice restaurants the most important thing in life? Was living in an extravagant home with a nice salary the ultimate pleasure? Or, was having my kids be sports heroes a worthy goal for which I should invest hours and hours of time and money? These goals were shallow, and never had I realized it more, than at that moment.

Suddenly, the decision was obvious. It was inconceivable for my family to leave the shul, our friends, or the commitment we had made towards learning about Judaism. Just as Lori had taught in her "48 Ways to Wisdom" class, based on the Gemara, that with much pleasure, comes much pain. Yes, there was pain, but hopefully, there would one day, please God, be pleasure.

As a result, Bob accepted an ER position, working at Ft. Carson in Colorado Springs. Although the drive was over an hour, the staff was supportive, the salary was adequate, and the job was fulfilling.

I decided that my goal in life had to be a close relationship with God, no matter what the cost. Bob and I continued to learn.

Shabbos became a day of the week that I looked forward to with great anticipation. The Jewish holidays became much more meaningful as I realized they each have a purpose. They were not created by Jews. They were created by God. Although I realized I couldn't "do it all", I could do my best out of my love for God. The traditions became less intimidating as I realized that they, too, have a purpose in giving the Jewish people identity and unity.

During the summer of 2004, Bob and I requested a date for our conversion with Rabbi Greenblatt of Memphis. The date was set for December 20, 2004, almost 10 years from the date we had the fateful meeting with the church members, asking us to leave the church.

A beis din was formed to witness our conversion. As the regular mikveh attendant was unable to be present the day of conversion, I needed a mikveh attendant. I asked the rabbis if it mattered who I chose. "Just someone you feel comfortable with." I chose Lori.

Bob and I began the preparation process for conversion. I needed a more formal review of the laws of family purity before immersing in the mikveh. We also had to explain the process of circumcision to our 6 year old son, Dakota. When he heard what circumcision entailed, he paused and quivering said, "Maybe I don't want to convert just yet." However, a close friend who had just gone through conversion months earlier, assured him that he would be okay—and he was.

Upon hearing the news of our conversion, many people would approach me and ask, "Are you excited?!!" "Yes", I would answer, I am excited. However, deep down inside, I felt a sense of trepidation as I knew the commitment and change came at great cost. Conversion was something I chose to do—not so much for the excitement, but for the relationship it would instill in me with my Eternal Creator.

As I prepared for conversion and the upcoming wedding, I experienced mixed emotions. I mourned for the relationship between me and my parents and how that would suffer even more. My parents were the ones who had given me life, raised and nurtured me, and now for this, my most important milestone, I could not joyfully share with them. I could not even find the words to tell them that I was converting! I knew the pain was great for them and did not wish to inflict any more than I already had.

On the other hand, I knew that conversion was right for me. Without it, I knew I would never be fulfilled in the way I desired. As painful or as different as it might have seemed for family or friends, it was still right for me and I had confidence that I was choosing the right path. So, it was with that confidence that I continued my chosen path towards conversion.

On Monday morning, December 20, 2004, Bob and I drove to West-side Denver, with Dakota and Danielle, for immersion into the mikveh that would forever change our lives.

Our son Stephen's conversion was placed on hold, based upon his decision to attend yeshiva. Up to this point, Stephen had only known a public school setting. If he chose not to attend yeshiva, then the rabbi did not want to perform his conversion. After careful consideration, Stephen chose yeshiva and his conversion was successfully completed nine months later. Rabbi Feldheim, the kind rabbi whom we had first met seven years earlier, became Stephen's rebbe for ninth grade and Lori Palatnik's son, Zev, was Stephen's dorm roommate.

The rabbis informed us that Dakota and Danielle would immerse in the mikveh the same day as Bob and me. If, however, upon Bar/Bat Mitzvah age, they decide not to be Jewish, their immersion in the mikveh would be considered null and void. On the other hand, if they wished to continue on their present path, they would then be given that right as converts.

When we arrived at the mikveh, the rabbis for the beis din were waiting for us. There was a minor delay as we waited for someone to arrive with the key to the mikveh. As we waited, Bob talked with the rabbis while I sat in Lori's van, talking and asking last minute questions about the mikveh. Finally, the moment arrived. The mikveh was unlocked and I was escorted into a room in which I was interviewed, one last time, by the beis din concerning my conversion. Rabbi Greenblatt reminded me that the Jewish people are a persecuted people and that there may very well be a second Holocaust. Was I prepared to suffer and endure the hardships so characteristic of the Jews? My answer was "yes". As Lori emphasized many times in her classes, "If you know what you're willing to die for, then you should also know what you're willing to live for." And yes, I wanted to live as a Jew. I was then taken back to the preparation room for the mikveh. As I showered and prepared, I kept thinking, "I hope I'm doing this right and I hope I can make it through the mikveh without drowning." While it is incumbent upon all Jews to learn to swim, I had never learned. My biggest exposure to water had been splashing around in the horse tanks on the farm. I was praying that I would somehow survive. When I finished my mikveh preparations, I "buzzed" Lori to come to room for a final inspection. She helped me with last minute preparations and then led me into the actual mikveh area. As I descended the steps into the warm water, a feeling of unbelievable love and comfort descended over me. I turned around to look at Lori, and with tears whispered, "I'm finally here. I'm finally here."

Lori smiled. "Now, why don't you just practice a few times going under the water?" she recommended.

Not knowing how to swim, I would get about three-fourths of the way under the water, then come back up, clinging to the sides of the mikveh. She would patiently respond, "Well, you're going to have to go all the way under and you can't cling to the sides."

After several attempts, she asked, "Would you like for me to get my swimsuit on and help you?"

"Yes!" I answered enthusiastically. "But then, how appropriate will that be for Lori to be wearing her swimsuit in front of all the rabbis?" I wondered to myself. "Won't that be rather immodest?"

My thoughts were soon put to rest when I laid eyes upon Lori's "swimsuit" which consisted of a long sleeve top and leggings covered by a skirt. "So, that's a Jewish swimsuit?" I thought with glee.

She descended into the water and helped me practice over and over again several times until I could finally immerse myself completely underwater and come up again.

There was soon a knock on the door as the rabbis asked if I was prepared. Lori told them I was. As they entered the room, Rabbi Meyer reminded me that as a convert, I would be obligated to keep all the commandments, even when they might seem difficult. As challenging as I knew it might be for me at times, I knew this is what I wanted. I responded, "Yes, I understand." I immersed and my conversion process was ruled complete.

"Mazel Tov!" the rabbis responded in unison. Lori and I embraced, as friends, and now as true Jewish sisters.

Next, Danielle proceeded into the mikveh. The immersion for her was much less traumatic because she had taken swimming lessons and liked the water. As she emerged from the mikveh, with a huge smile, we hugged.

After Danielle and I dressed and proceeded from the building, Bob and Dakota, were waiting for us, new converts, as well. However, we were no longer Bob, Marcella, Danielle and Dakota. As new creations, we were now to be known as Yedidyah, Leah, Esther and Binyamin.

Bob chose the name Yedidyah because of its meaning for Solomon: beloved of God. Many years earlier, he had wanted to name our first born son, Robbie, Jedidiah. I balked at the idea, saying that I didn't want our son's nickname to be Jed. It reminded me too much of Jed Clampitt from the Beverly Hillbillies. However, Bob loved the name and finally took it for himself.

I chose the name Leah because of her Biblical traits. She was known to have "weak eyes" from crying. Through my spiritual journey, I too, had suffered "weak eyes". Leah was blessed with four sons. I, also, was blessed with four sons. I admired Leah as a Jewish matriarch and wanted her name as my own.

Danielle chose the name Esther because Esther was a queen. Danielle wanted to be viewed as a girl with a queen-like demeanor.

Dakota chose the name Binyamin because he liked the name and felt it was appropriate. Just as Binyamin was the youngest son of Jacob, Dakota was also the youngest son in his family.

Immediately following the conversion, Jewish law required that Yedidyah and I be remarried as new converts. For the rest of the day, we were not allowed to touch each other until after the wedding. We were also required to fast for the day. Unlike my first Yom Kippur experience, I was able to not eat anything this time.

The ceremony took place that evening, December 20, 2004, and was officiated by Rabbi Meyer. Because Bob and I had only attended two Jewish weddings in our lifetime, we needed help. Therefore, Lori obtained a tape of Jane and Serge Herscovici's wedding so that we could review it together and understand what to do. "The main thing," Lori advised, is just know when to say "Amen".

As I walked down the shul aisle that evening, accompanied on one side by Lori, and the other by Chaya Meyer, I felt a tremendous sense of gratitude and joy. I admired both Lori and Chaya so much and felt incredibly honored that they would walk me towards my new chossen.

As I gazed at Yedidyah, standing at the front of the shul, I could see tears in his eyes. I, too, began to cry, but this time, they were tears of intense, indescribable joy. The shul was filled with our friends, standing in our honor, most teary-eyed, as well. We had finally come home: to our faith, our love, and our friends. "Pain before pleasure", Lori taught. Pleasure had finally come.

41

Weeks earlier, when Bob and I discussed our wedding, we decided upon a short ceremony in Rabbi Meyer's office. However, the members of the shul, especially the women, encouraged us to have a "real wedding" in the sanctuary, followed by a reception. Vicki Olesky, a woman who befriended us, even while in Colorado Springs, agreed to host a reception at her home. She prepared a yummy meal of meatballs and rice and fresh fruit, (something even our kids would eat!) as well as a beautiful wedding cake. Other women pitched in by baking desserts and other delicacies. It was a beautiful reception, but more importantly than that, I experienced an incredible feeling of acceptance and love and warmth within the Jewish community. God had given me friends who were also now family.

Ironically enough, 20 years earlier, when selecting an inscription for the groom's cake at our Christian wedding, Bob and I chose the following verse from Ruth,

"Whither thou goest, I will go, and where thou lodgest, I will lodge: thy people shall be my people and thy God my God." "Thy people shall be my people and thy God, my God." I loved the verse when it was inscribed on the cake, but now it has been inscribed on my life.

The following Shabbos after our conversion, Yedidyah and I sponsored the Kiddush at shul, the date: December 25, 2004.

Was the pain worth it? Yes—a hundred, million times yes! For over 40 years, I searched for the missing link—what would bring completeness, what would give me that relationship I yearned for so much with my Creator. For the first time in my life, since conversion, I feel complete. The missing link has been found. There is an indescribable sense of wholeness. I feel as though I have finally returned home to a God who is Real, who hears my prayers, and loves me with an amazing unconditional love. "God, I really want to know You—whatever the cost. Whatever it takes, please lead me into a deeper and more meaningful relationship with You." Be careful what you pray for. You just might get it!

ABOUT THE AUTHOR

Leah Schiermeyer was the prototypical "good Christian girl". Raised in rural Oklahoma, the center of the Bible Belt, she was steeped in fundamental, evangelical Christian teachings. Her great grandfather was a Baptist preacher and her father was a lay leader in their small country church. She embraced the faith of her fathers with a fervor and zeal that would have made any revival preacher proud. She knew nothing of Jews except what she had read in the Bible or had heard from the pulpit. She never met a practicing Jew until she was well into adulthood. She was a shy, reserved young girl who found herself abandoning the faith of her family and friends in favor of a religion that she knew almost nothing about, and what she had heard, was quite negative. As a dedicated Christian, the path to Judaism for her was a long, and sometimes arduous one, but one well worth the journey.

Wedding Day, November 17, 1984.

My Three Sons: Robbie (background), Michael, and Stephen.

In spite of my illness, God blessed me with two healthy babies.

My Three Sons, joined by twins: Dakota and Danielle.

Lori became my friend, my confidante, and eventually, my Jewish sister.

Our 2nd Wedding Day, December 20, 2004 (9 Teves 5765.)

Binyamin (Dakota) celebrated his bar mitzvah on his Hebrew birthday, 18 Teves, (December 25, 2010.)

GLOSSARY

ba'al teshuva: one who returns; newly observant Jew. It is often contrasted with "FFB" (Frum From Birth), which refers to Orthodox Jews who are born into families that are already religiously observant and have been practicing Judaism from birth.

bar/bat mitzvah: (bar is son; bat is daughter) refers, technically, to the children who are coming of age. At age 13, (12 for girls), children become obligated to observe the commandments. More commonly the term is used to refer to the coming of age ceremony itself.

beis din: the ruling authority of the Rabbinical court, or a group of three Rabbis.

blech: metal sheet used by many observant Jews to cover stovetop burners, as part of the precautions taken to avoid violating the prohibition against cooking on the Sabbath.

challah: a bread leavened with yeast and containing eggs; often made into braided loaves, prepared especially for the Jewish Sabbath.

chassidic: sect of Judaism whose dress is often characterized by long black coats and black hats.

chossen: Yiddush term for a Jewish groom

circumsion: removal of the foreskin, a commandment in Judaism performed on the 8th day of a male child's life or upon conversion to Judaism. Referred to in Yiddish as a bris.

davening: Yiddish term for prayer. Observant Jews daven three times a day in addition to reciting blessings over many other common activities.

David Hamelech: King David

gefilte fish: poached fish patties or fish balls made from a mixture of ground deboned fish, mostly carp or pike.

Gemara: part of the Talmud (collection of ancient rabbinic writings on Jewish civil and religious law) that contains commentary on the Mishnah, part of the Oral Law of the Jewish religion.

HaShem: God.

Havadalah: a ritual marking the end of Shabbos (the Sabbath) or a holiday.

kashrut: set of Jewish dietary laws

kiddush: blessing recited over wine or grape juice to sanctify the Shabbos and Jewish holidays. Kiddush also refers to refreshments or light meals served at the synagogue following prayer services on Shabbos or holidays, which begin with the recitation of the Kiddush blessing.

kiruv shul: shul who practices bringing secularized Jews closer to Judaism, especially Orthodox Judaism, as through seminars, meetings and religious rituals.

kugels: Jewish baked dish, usually made of noodles or potatoes, baked until crusty. Some kugels contain fruit or other vegetables.

lashon hara: sins against other people committed by speech, such as defamation, gossip, swearing falsely, and scoffing.

matzah: unleavened bread traditionally served during Passover.

matzah pizza: a flat, open-faced pizza, consisting of a matza crust topped with tomato sauce and cheese.

matzo ball: Jewish dumpling made with matzo meal and served in soup.

Mazel Tov: Literally the Hebrew words for good luck, but usually means Congratulations!

mikveh: bath used for the ritual immersion in Judaism

mitzvah: good deed; commandment, Jewish law of moral conduct

parsha: a weekly Torah portion read in synagogue.

peyos: long sideburns worn by traditional Jewish men in observance of the commandment in Leviticus 19:27 not to round the corners of the head or the beard. Because there are points of Jewish law that allow some shaving, some Orthodox Jews do not have full beards or peyos.

rebbe: rabbi, teacher

rebbetzen: wife of a rabbi

seder: a Jewish ritual feast that marks the beginning of the Jewish holiday of Passover. The Seder is a ritual performed by a community or by multiple generations of a family, involving a retelling of the story of the liberation of the Israelites from slavery in ancient Egypt. The seder itself is based on the Biblical verse commanding Jews to retell the story of the Exodus from Egypt. Seder customs include drinking four cups of wine, eating matzah and partaking of symbolic foods placed on the Passover Seder Plate.

Shabbaton: A Shabbos, usually designated with out of town speakers and a special meal usually served at the shul.

shalom bayis: Hebrew word, literally meaning peace in the home.

shalosh seudos: the third meal customarily eaten by Sabbath-observing Jews on Shabbos.

shul: the Yiddish term for a Jewish house of worship (synagogue).

succah: temporary hut constructed during the week-long Jewish festival of Succot. It is topped with branches and often decorated with autumn or Judaic themes. The book of Leviticus describes it as a symbolic wilderness shelter, commemorating the time God provided for the Israelites in the wilderness after they were freed from slavery in Egypt.

Succos (or Succot): a festival commemorating the wandering in the desert and the final harvest.

Tay Sachs: deadly disease of the nervous system passed down through families. About 1 in every 27 members of the Ashkenazi Jewish population carries the Tay Sachs gene.

Torah: In its narrowest sense, Torah is the first five books of the Bible: Genesis, Exodus, Leviticus, Numbers and Deuteronomy. In its broadest sense, Torah is the entire body of Jewish teachings.

treif: food that is not in accordance with Jewish laws

yarmulke: a man's skullcap, worn especially during prayer and religious study

yeshiva: an Orthodox Jewish school of higher instruction in Jewish learning.

yom tov: Jewish holiday

Made in the USA
Middletown, DE
01 July 2015